CONTENTS

The Schwarzkopf Tapes

An artist replies to a hostile biography

Edited by Alan Sanders

Classical Recordings Quarterly
&
The Elisabeth Schwarzkopf/Walter Legge Society

Published by Classical Recordings Quarterly
&
The Elisabeth Schwarzkopf/Walter Legge Society © 2010

ISBN 978-0-9567361-0-9

Design & DTP by Jiří Musil of S2DO Ltd
Printed by Manson Group

INTRODUCTION

In the early part of 1996 a biography of Elisabeth Schwarzkopf by the British writer Alan Jefferson was published. The book provoked widespread critical attention, much of it hostile to Schwarzkopf; for here, apparently, was confirmation of the singer's previously rumoured complicity with the Nazi regime during the early years of her career.

In his foreword to the book Jefferson states that he approached Dame Elisabeth for her cooperation in his work, but was rejected. The pages which follow this introduction reproduce the letters concerned, as well as later correspondence between Schwarzkopf and the publisher. Readers can thus make up their own minds as to whether Jefferson did actually make the approach in the way he relates.

Soon after the book's publication Dame Elisabeth asked me to travel to her home in Zumikon, near Zürich, so that I could go through the book with her. She had recently undergone an eye operation, which made lengthy concentration on the printed word difficult, and my task was thus to read the text to her, and to note her comments. There is no doubt that at this time she had every intention of taking legal action against some of the book's allegations. Also present was Lily Reenvig, Elisabeth's Danish friend of many years. Lily had spent a long career in the record retailing trade, and was a great authority on any matter concerning the singer's performances and recordings.

At our first sessions, on 13 and 14 April 1996, a tape recorder was used to capture my reading aloud and Schwarzkopf's reactions. As readers will gather from the transcripts, the contents of the book's early pages caused her to become angry and distressed at that fact that material she regarded as incorrect or misleading had become fixed in print. I arrived at her house early on 15 April in order to continue our work, and she told me that she was not able not continue the exercise: I was booked to fly back to England three days later and she asked me to take a break at her expense until the time came for my departure.

Three months later, I was back in Zumikon. Elisabeth had changed her mind and now wished to complete her exploration of the book's contents. Several sessions, more lengthy than before, took place between 6 and 10 July. We went through the book as before, but unfortunately a recorder was not available this time, and my records of those sessions only survive in the form of written notes. Though Schwarzkopf's antipathy to the book's content and presentation was then as strong as it had been before, my notes only recorded her general reactions and not the pungency of her responses as conveyed by the recordings. I have therefore decided to note important factual errors only from the later part of the book and these form Part 3 of this publication.

To the concern of many of her friends and admirers, Elisabeth was persuaded not to take legal action against the book, on the grounds that it would be too expensive and too long a procedure for someone of her age to undertake. Some observers regarded her lack of defence as indicating that Jefferson's accusations had been accurate, and thus the printed word has effectively, in this case as in so many others, become "gospel".

I retained possession of the April 1996 tapes, and have for some years wondered how they might be used to counter Jefferson's book. Late last year action finally became possible when Dr Daphne Kerslake, Chair of the Elisabeth Schwarzkopf/ Walter Legge Society generously offered to transcribe the recordings. This provided an ideal solution to the problem, since Daphne's knowledge of Dame Elisabeth and her work has enabled her to provide an admirably accurate and faithful transcription throughout a very time-consuming and demanding exercise.

Though fluent in English, Elisabeth used the language less at the age of 80 than at an earlier part of her life, when she had lived in London and was married to an Englishman. Sometimes her use of words and phrase was now idiosyncratic: the meaning is usually clear enough, however, and we have not attempted to correct her English. She also tended to use words repetitively – the word "silly" crops up very frequently, for instance. Daphne's task was also not made easier by the fact that Elisabeth spoke very quickly, even in a second language. The printed text reproduces the recording as closely as possible: some words we haven't been able to catch, however – particularly names of individuals.

One or two friends have suggested that it would be better not to publish this document; to "let sleeping dogs lie". Our response is that this tactic has not worked in the years since the publication of Jefferson's book, because every so often, when Schwarzkopf's name comes up, the same old allegations accompany it. Apart from her reactions to the text, Elisabeth was stimulated to reminisce about her early years, and much of this material is new to our knowledge of her. Perhaps the publication of this goes a little against her view, stated at the beginning of the transcription, that artists' lives should not be investigated, and that only their art is relevant, but there is nothing very private in her recorded memories. And it was clear at the time that our exercise was not just for her own private use, but that our findings would be employed to reach a wider audience and form part of the then intended legal action.

The tapes show Schwarzkopf's directness and toughness of character, her willingness to acknowledge honestly her own strengths and weaknesses, and her sense of humour even in such a stressful undertaking. Most important of all is the revelation of her father's clash with the Nazis, the results of which had far-reaching consequences for Elisabeth and her parents. (I have introduced an explanatory note at the point where these issues crop up). Nowhere else are these facts to be found – they have been completely (and maybe conveniently) overlooked by her critics.

One final comment on the dialogue. It occurs to me now that I was sometimes guilty of encouraging a negative response in Elisabeth's reactions; of pointing out and underlining aberrations in the written text. I was then very caught up in what seemed to be an unfair and biased account of a life and I should probably have been more dispassionate in my role.

Alan Jefferson died in April 2010 at the age of 89. It may seem that we have waited for his death before publishing our document, but this is not so. We would have much preferred him to be able to read Dame Elisabeth's reactions to his work. The timing is coincidental.

Alan Sanders, October 2010

HOW IT ALL BEGAN

2 May 1991

Deviock Farm House
Deviock,   Torpoint
Cornwall   PL11 3DL

Dr.Elisabeth Legge-Schwarzkopf
Kammersängerin
Rebhusstrasse 29
CH-8126 ZUMIKON
Switzerland

Dear Madam Schwarzkopf

It has saddened many people that there has not, so far, been an authoritative biography of yourself. This week, I was asked by a firm of London publishers whether I thought you might be agreeable to discussing the matter.

While I cannot claim more than a passing acquaintanceship with you, via Walter, please do not regard this as an intrusion: I am merely being a Bote.

Yours sincerely

Alan Jefferson

Note from Alan Jefferson to Elisabeth Schwarzkopf

Mr. Alan Jefferson
Deviock Farm House

<u>Deviock</u>   Torpoint
<u>Cornwall</u>   PL11 3DL

England

                                                6.5.91

Dear Mr. Jefferson,

Many thanks for your information that a firm in London
would be interested to publish my biography.

I am so sorry to have already given the rights for
any book I might write to Faber & Faber, namely the
firm which so bravely published my book about Mr. Walter
Legge.

Thank you again for being the "Bote".

Kindest regards,

Yours sincerely

Prof. Dr. Elisabeth Legge-Schwarzkopf
Kammersängerin

Elisabeth Schwarzkopf's reply

Dr. Elisabeth Legge-Schwarzkopf, Kammersängerin

Rebhusstrasse 29, CH-8126 Zumikon, Tel. Zürich 01/918 22 83

13. 8. 92.

Publications Director
of Victor Gallancz Ltd.
14, Henrietta Street,
London W.C.2.

Dear Sir,

I have been informed that you
intend to make my life and work
the subject of a book. I was told
you have asked Mr. Alan Jefferson
to undertake the research and writing
of this publication.

Your intention certainly is very
flattering to me, but may I be
allowed to express my extreme
annoyance — to say the least — that
neither you nor Mr. Jefferson up to
now turned to me in the first
place for my permission to launch
such a project plus its necessary
research.

You will certainly understand
that I want to protect the author
as much as myself against
possibly erroneous reporting — and

10

its consequences — , although I
assume it would be intended to be
in my best interest.

Therefore I would be grateful if
you would be so good as to let me
have details of the sources of information, on which your writer will
base his work — should it come to
publication.

Yours sincerely
Elisabeth Legge Schwarzkopf
D.B.E.

Copy to Mr. Alan Jefferson
Copy to Mr. Charles Rodier, EMI, London.

Elisabeth Schwarzkopf's letter to Gollancz

ALAN JEFFERSON
DEVIOCK FARM HOUSE
DEVIOCK, TORPOINT
CORNWALL PL11 3DI

17 August 1992

Dear Dame Elisabeth,

This is to acknowledge the copy letter from you which arrived on 15th.

I am certain that you will be hearing from Victor Gollancz Ltd.

Yours sincerely

Alan Jefferson

Acknowledgement by Alan Jefferson

Victor Gollancz Ltd

14 HENRIETTA STREET
LONDON WC2E 8QJ
TELEPHONE 071-836 2006/2515
TELEX 265033   FAX 071-379 0934

19 August 1992

Dr. Elisabeth Legge-Schwarzkopf DBE
Rebhusstrasse 29
CH 8126 Zumikon
Switzerland

Dear Dame Elisabeth

Thank you for your letter of 13 August which the publishing director passed
on to me, as I commissioned Alan Jefferson to write your biography for Victor
Gollancz.

If you remember, Mr. Jefferson wrote to you in the spring of last year asking
if you would cooperate in a biography of yourself. You replied that you did
not wish to be involved with such a project. Although we respected your
decision, Mr. Jefferson and I felt, after consideration, that we should still
like to proceed with a biography. You are, after all, one of the most celebrated
of the post-war sopranos, and many opera and Lieder lovers would be keen to
read a detailed account of your career.

Mr. Jefferson is an accomplished and experienced writer on music, especially
singers (his most recent book is a biography of Lotte Lehmann) and has a close
knowledge of your art, on record and from live performances. We have every
confidence he will do justice to your career. His research for the biography
has taken him to archives in Berlin, Vienna and Milan; in addition he has talked
to a number of people who have known you personally.

I hope this goes some way to reassuring you that we and Mr. Jefferson have every
intention in producing a properly researched and accurate account of your
distinguished career.

Yours sincerely

Richard Wigmore
Associate Editor

Letter from Gollancz

FOREWORD

AS: *Foreword. Dame Elisabeth Schwarzkopf's many admirers in the musical world must often have wondered over the years at the absence of a substantial biography which this celebrated twentieth-century soprano demands.*

ES: Yes, I want to tell you something – I have never ever wanted anybody to look into my private life because I think it is some kind of voyeurism. It is wanting to peer into people's private life. What matters is the performances I did and the records I did. And that is all. They should know who I am from those things and not from of any kind of silly stories from home life or whatever it is. I have always refused, as you know, to do the story of my life – I also refused because I can't write a story, I am not one of those. But it is quite abhorrent to me, as much as it is abhorrent to me that people come to me physically, you know when we are standing in a queue for passport for coming into the country and they come and queue up and they are very near to me and every time I turn round and say to the next man, "Please don't breathe down my neck", or if they don't understand I stare them back. I cannot bear it. I cannot bear to be touched an awful lot – I never could, so that's one of my drawbacks, perhaps and perhaps it is also an advantage, I am sure. But I cannot, I cannot have people looking into my private life. No. Never could – before all that happened.

AS: *In 1990, I passed on to Dr Schwarzkopf, as she then was, the message from Gollancz that they would like to commission her autobiography or a biography.*
Well, we know that's not true.

ES: But there wasn't this…what is that letter?

AS: The letter just says that he talked to a London publisher about doing a biography. It wasn't put in such definite terms as that, not anywhere.

AS: *She was disinclined to accept the invitation, however, and one could only hope that as she had reached the age of 75, some means of persuading her to alter her decision would be found. It would be regrettable if the details of this remarkable woman's life were not to become widely known after such a spectacular career on the opera stage, in the concert hall, the recital room and the recording studio.*

ES: Yes, and I only have to say – why would it be regrettable? For whom? For whom? I don't *want* it to be known. No. Why should they? It is now the fashion, I know that, but I have all kinds of singers' books standing here and do you think I have I looked into one of them? I don't want to peer into the other peoples' lives and I will not.

AS: *When living persons supervise the writing of their own memoirs, they are bound to have recollections and information unavailable elsewhere, ...*

ES: Hopefully! [laughs]

AS: *... especially concerning childhood and family matters, not to mention retrospective and mature views about their own formative years, On the other hand ...*

ES: That is all utterly silly! Because what matters is the *result* of those formative years, not the formative years as such. It is nobody's business to know about it. What matters is what the result is and I am the first one to criticise myself when the result is not to my liking or to my expectations. I know it better than any audience what isn't good, you see. And I am really quite open to say "no" about it. And it is the result that matters. Not the way up there.

AS: *On the other hand, nobody will want to divulge every past event or association, especially those of a deeply personal nature.*

ES: Ahh! Hear, hear!

AS: *A biography that is dependent upon the approval of the subject ...*

ES: We come back on to the page where it says "the three pairs of shoes". Oh God, the silly ape – I am sorry!

AS: *A biography that is dependant on the approval of the subject may reveal many obscure and important details; but it will almost certainly be highly selective.*
    In Dame Elisabeth's case there is no established public archive relating to her life and career, ...

ES: Well, it cannot be, because I took from Berlin a rucksack which contained a lot of music – we didn't have photocopiers at that time so we had to take the volumes with us plus one evening dress, the one which I always wore which was made by my grandmother, plus a skirt which was given to me by [Maria] Ivogün so I could do concerts, and some shoes and the things which belong to all this and that is what I had to carry with me, getting out of – it wasn't bombed totally but I couldn't get back into the house, so I couldn't take anything else, you see.

AS: *... although material is held in a dozen different opera houses, city libraries and other collections. In going it alone without the advantage of Schwarzkopf's help, I have been fortunate in receiving a great deal of willing assistance from outside sources.*

ES: Well he shouldn't complain, because we have a letter where he doesn't want to ask me, you see. If he would have asked me he would have had another result surely, and maybe I would have thrown him out in five minutes. So there you are.

16

AS: *The Schwarzkopf-Legge Society of London circulates useful information about her to its members; many newspaper and magazine interviews, minuscule biographies and a whole issue devoted to Schwarzkopf in the excellent L'Avant-Scène l'Opéra series have also been published.*

ES: What's that?

AS: I don't know what that is – *L'Avant-Scène.*

LR: That would be the one published with the *Les Introuvables* – it came out in France.

ES: Oh, *Les Introuvables* – it could be, yes. There were some details. But they were also not right. No. So!

AS: *There is a fine book of photographs with brief but vital text by an Italian critic and a short monograph…*

ES: And the details are not right. They are not right, they are not accurate. They are not consistent, all of them: they issued wrong statements as for instance the Adele in Paris which is a damaging statement to me at the time, because I wouldn't have taken that important role to an outside guest performance of the opera, which was very important for them surely, if in the role up to then had happened – that was the little Eva who has to sing, I believe, two sentences solo – all the other things are ensemble.

AS: *… and a short monograph with some family photographs, written by the music critic of a French newspaper in the 1950s.*

ES: What was that? Oh! Yes.

AS: *Then there is her own On and Off the Record, a tribute to Walter Legge that also contains a good deal about herself.*

ES: Does it? I wonder.

AS: Well, there is Walter's piece about you.

ES: Well yes, that's true. Yes.

AS: *In the middle of the 1950s I spent a convivial day with the Legges.*

ES: Where? When? That – he can say it, but surely not with the Legges, it was not me, maybe he did it with Mr Legge? I don't know. I wasn't there a lot of the time. He never mentioned the name, he never told me that there was such a man about. I met him only in the memorial service to Walter on 6 June when he stood with my relatives, Walter's sister and her husband and the children and stood next to them when I was going out of the – what is it called again?

LR: St James's.

ES: St James's, yes. And as I saw them standing together I said, "Of course, you are all coming along, all of you", without addressing anybody personally, you see, which he did and he then must have. Of course we then shook hands, surely, which I don't remember – there were quite a lot of people in the Connaught Hotel. I hope I will stand all this, you know.

AS: Well, if it is too much, please say.

AS: *Then, during the last three years of Walter Legge's life, he and I met in London a number of times.*

ES: Which was? Doing what?

AS: *Then, during the last three years …*

ES: Oh no, no, he must have met him once there, when Walter was in the Connaught. But that wasn't in the last three years, that was in the last two years of Walter's life and that makes a lot of difference – somebody with that ailment, you see.

AS: *In between these meetings, Legge and I frequently exchanged letters that covered all manner of musical subjects; …*

ES: Oh no, it was only on Beecham and it is here, he was writing a book on Beecham – I haven't seen it – but he has and my husband was writing an article on Beecham in the last six months of his life. I have to find out from Margaret [Pacy] because I think she typed it. It was very difficult for him. He took great pains and had great difficulty to do that article at all. I don't know it was for a magazine…

AS: *Gramophone.*

ES: …because he had worked under Beecham, with Beecham, you see in all those years in Covent Garden. And I have here only three responses of Walter – you will come to it where he says Walter had bidden him to destroy all those letters, which I cannot believe.

AS: *… but, less than a month before he died, he insisted that I destroy them. I have drawn on my memory to resurrect some of his views and anecdotes.*

ES: That is not fair. Because he can say it and I am sure it isn't true. From the letters there are of Walter, they are frankly coolish, cool of standing, yes, some acquaintance who deals with music – and since he had nobody to write to and nobody to talk to, he did. It was this kind of thing being alone, with not having anybody there to discuss musical matters, so he did it to this man whom he didn't even mention to me – I had no idea who that was.

AS: Then he goes on simply to list people who helped – so I don't think we need to go into that, do we?

ES: Who would they be?

AS: Well, mostly people you would never have heard of.

ES: Well we'll see. I can't see it as I don't have the right glasses.

AS: Do you want me to read the names out?

ES: Yes.

AS: *The following individuals greatly assisted me, on a personal basis, while I was writing this book: Thaddeus Crenshaw, Paris; Karin Heckermann, Berlin, Eliot Levin, New Barnet; Christopher Norton-Welsh, Vienna; and James Seddon, London. Gale Andrews, Watford; Felix Aprahamian, London...*

ES: Well, he was a critic, wasn't he?

AS: *Julian Budden, Florence; George Clare, Suffolk; Lord Donaldson, London...*

ES; Yes, he was acquainted with them – with the Donaldsons.

AS: *Mathias Erhard, Berlin; Niklas Frank, Hamburg; Michael Gasson, London; Guido Hausmann, Düsseldorf; John Hunt, London...*

ES: Is that John Hunt who...Aha!

AS: *Floris Juynboll, Nieuwegein; Frau Lotte Klemperer, Zollikon; Brian Lamport, Salzburg; Alfred Levy, Bournemouth; Isadore Lichtman, Chicago; Bernard Pallut, London; Ivor Pfuell, London; Henry Pleasants, London ...*

ES: Yes, he was something in Vienna after the war, with the...something to do with Vienna with concerts from the American...well perhaps it was not the army, it was some kind of American person after the war in Vienna. I think there's a photograph I've got with him somewhere standing after a concert, yes.

AS: *Gerald L. Posner, New York; Dr Oliver Rathkolb, Vienna; Michael Scott, Rome, David Vick, Isle of Man and Dr Edward Wrzesien, Warsaw.*

ES: These ones I don't know at all – I have heard the names.

AS: *The following individuals and their organisations were most helpful, and deserve special thanks: Frau Edda Facklam, Pilz Music, Hamburg; Frau Karin Heckermann and Herr Curt Roesler, Städtische Oper, Berlin; Dr Dagmar Wünsche, Akademie der Künste, Berlin; Dr Peter Andry, Warner Classics International, London...*

ES: We know him, yes!

[AS continues to read the names of those who had provided assistance – as listed on page 10 of the book.]

Also to the following archivists and librarians: D. Aubrey, Archives SB Monte Carlo ... [the list as read continues on to page 11].

ES: It is all the librarians of all the places I ever stood on the stage, or something.

AS: *As well as to those solely connected with the cinema: Robert Hoffmann, Munich; Laurent Lyons, TPA, Wiesbaden; Wolfgang Theis, Stiftung Deutsche Kinemathek, Berlin; British Film Institute, London; Deutsche Institut für Filmkunde, Frankfurt; Friedrich- Wilhelm-Murnau Stiftung, Wiesbaden.*

ES: I wonder how much he paid all these people – or Gollancz? They must have had a lot of money – to pay all those connections – and surely he must have been going to some places, you know. Do you listen, Lily? Do you know any?

LR: No.

PREFACE

AS: Now we come on to the Preface.

ES: Thank you! Oh, here we go!

AS: *To many lovers of fine singing over the age of 35, Elisabeth Schwarzkopf in concert is still vividly recalled in the mind's eye, standing in a bright light beside the piano, the embodiment of femininity, gorgeously groomed and dressed. We remember how we applauded vigorously while waiting impatiently for her …*

ES: It is already an offence to write a book with this kind of beginning which thinks there is something good coming. But it isn't, it is destroying me completely – he was, and then he starts like that. I find that the falsest thing I have ever heard as an attitude of a person.

AS: *… while waiting impatiently for her to fill the hall with her own special luxury of soprano singing.*

ES: And by the way, I want to it make it clear why I had the bright light because I didn't want to see the public, for that and no other reason. I also, who sang all the time in front of non-German speaking public, I wanted them to read my lips as much as they could, but it was mainly to make me blind against the public because on some occasions I couldn't have the light in my eyes and I saw people sitting everywhere waving their fans as in Turin, or some chauffeur in the highest degree in Rome reading their paper or somebody in Copenhagen sleeping quite frankly and not applauding and all those things I didn't want to see. And quite soon I have this – they all copied me afterwards and they had the light into their eyes which I am paying now for, you see, with my eyes, and frankly because we had the light on in the audience so they could read the translations and Walter took very great pains on translations, as you know, with mostly William Mann and very often himself with me and that was a very, very important thing on the very difficult programmes which Walter presented. He did it not only with me but with every artist who sang for him. He prepared the translations and looked them through and it was quite out of the question that the hall was maybe dark. It would also not be the principle of a Lieder recital. A Lieder recital is in principle that one person out of the audience who happens to have the voice and the art sings, not the opera where it is two worlds on which the public looks upon with drawn curtains – it is a different principle altogether.

AS: *The programmes were always a skilful juxtaposition of the mournful and the contemplative, the cheerful and the humorous …*

21

ES: I'll tell you what that is about. There are, for soprano voices like me – there are no, how do say, like *Winterreise* and *Müllerin* – no cycles, apart from *Frauenliebe und Leben* that I did sing at the end of my professional career and bad it was – that is the only cycle really apart from the Stuart songs which is a cycle in its way, and that is for a mezzo-soprano. So you had to make something of a totally different programme. Also I was no longer very much in my very first few years, as we know, when I did the big concerts I had to be careful that my voice was very much changing from high to low, from soft to loud all the time changed, not ever hammering into one realm of the voice or one kind of loudness, so it had to be, for technical reasons, for health of the voice, the programmes had to be made that way. Besides, a recital is also, and Walter was – I know he was of that opinion – that it should also be an entertainment, not entertainment of today, no, but it should really kindle the people's fantasy and thinking and feelings – but was an entertainment, not just a religious service.

AS: ... and, just occasionally grotesquely comic, and they were always perfectly delivered. In Elisabeth Schwarzkopf's heyday each event was a magnet for lovers of distinguished singing from all over the world. Happily, much of Schwarzkopf's wide repertoire has been carefully preserved on disc, not only the Lieder at which she excelled, but also her major operatic roles which, for two decades after the war, she played on all the great stages of the Western world. Few London opera lovers under 50 will have seen Schwarzkopf there for her last appearances at the Royal Opera House were as Strauss's Marschallin in 1959.

ES: Where?

AS: At the Opera House.

ES: My last appearance?

LR: *Rosenkavalier* with Solti.

ES: My last appearance on any stage?

AS: No, in Covent Garden.

ES: Was it with Solti – *Rosenkavalier*? – unfortunately with Solti, yes!

AS: *As an opera singer she is still spoken of with reverence at the Vienna State Opera, at Salzburg and at La Scala Milan. In the United States she is remembered more in San Francisco where she made her American debut than at the New York Met with which her relations were chequered.*

ES: I hope so, because I was awful, sure!

AS: *Schwarzkopf's career was extraordinary because it involved so much travel and so many appearances. It was a quadruple life in the opera house, the concert hall, the recital room and the recording studio from city to city and continent to continent.*

ES: Any idiot can see that, you know. I don't have to have a writer to say *that* for God's sake. Honestly – any person who comes to a concert can know that without it even being written down, for Christ's sake.

AS: *From the 1960s onward, Lieder recitals increasingly dominated her career until she gave her farewell recital in March 1979 at the age of 63. She did not ...*

ES: Where was that?

AS: Zürich.

ES: At the age of 63. When was it? '79 – of course. '79, '79 – I was 64 it must have been, I would have been 63. Wait a minute.

LR: It was March '79.

ES: March '79. But I am born in ...

LR: December '15.

ES: That's what I can't get together myself ... now how is this again, hold it, hold it, hold it ...

LR: 63, because it was in March '79.

ES: OK, 63.

AS: *But she did not retire altogether. Masterclasses, private pupils, seminars and competitions continued to occupy her well past her seventy-fifth birthday in 1990. By then she had received more honours and decorations than any other singer. If one asks how all this came about, the answer lies in two words: talent and ambition. She grasped ...*

ES: Ambition I refuse. I refuse. I wasn't ambitious. I wanted to *sing*. And I never asked for to sing anywhere, it all came to me without asking of me. Never. The only time I gave an audition was for Berlin. That was the only audition I ever gave apart from the one for Clemens Krauss who didn't take me, said I wasn't good enough for Munich at the time. That was in Berlin in the Staatsoper – when was it, Lily? An audition I had to sing for Clemens Krauss who wanted to engage me for the Munich Opera – and he wanted to hear me; he had heard about me. I went to the Staatsoper, I think he accompanied himself and his daughter was in the next room, who also heard me singing. He looked in there after the singing, looked in that room and then turned round and said, "Well, I don't think you are quite yet needed for us in Munich". I don't know when it was, I can't give you the year.

Anyway, the gist of the matter was that certainly his wife wasn't there and I must tell you that same wife was the one who, in an alarm in Vienna, when we were with my mother for that little month when we were put into the Vienna Imperial Hotel. There was an alarm and I had two suit cases and my mother also had a broken arm still – she was suffering from it – and we actually went to the elevator that took us down into the very entrails of down, down under – you know Vienna has very many lower gangways where the people survived and somebody out of the elevator grabbed at my two suitcases and said, "You can't do that alone, come on let me carry it", and it was Mrs Clemens Krauss who was also there. Yes, she was quite a woman, I dare say. Ja.

Viorica Ursuleac, soprano, the wife
of Clemens Krauss

AS: *She grasped and nurtured the seed of a talent which had been born in her, willed it to flower through sheer determined hard work.*

ES: Well "sheer determined" – that is what is wrong and what people from nowadays from hindsight say, to make a career. The word career was not known to us, we wanted to *sing*. That was all there was, you see. And learning how to sing well, and how to perform with orchestras, and how to perform in opera and how to perform in all the realms of music which there are available for a soprano. That isn't even so many – a mezzo has many more, you see. So there. And that word is really quite from me because it was drilled into me from the beginning; never, never, never to use one's elbows to make a career. I was only using the way I sang. And the musicality I had, the sight-reading possibility, the stage possibility – which I had, I wasn't bad, obviously, or any young years on the stage to do those things which were given to me, not asked for, given to me to do them well. So there. And I was always frightened that I wasn't good enough. Always. Through my whole life. That goes with me like a shadow all the time. Oh, it wasn't good enough. Oh no. The only thing I thought good enough at one time was a performance with Krips in Chicago of Fiordiligi where he beamed such joy about what I did on stage that that alone made you feel well, you see. No, I think when I sang with Boskovsky – those were the absolutely physical well-being moments of singing.

AS: *… and sought no alternatives in life except that would make it bloom even more richly. Elisabeth Schwarzkopf faced few professional setbacks once she had passed a single audition for the Berlin Deutsche Oper during Holy Week in April 1938.*

ES. On Wednesday.

AS: *There had been a disturbing passage with an inappropriate singing teacher at the beginning of her formal vocal training; but once …*

ES: No, no that should be because I had to learn the part of the second Blumenmädchen, first group, alone with my *clavier* in the night from Wednesday to Thursday and then I had all Thursday to learn and then Friday morning I had a *clavier* rehearsal in the opera with not the conductor for the evening but somebody, not with the other Blumenmädchen but alone, and then there was an evening show, never having been on a big stage at all or having been singing with a big orchestra ever and then I was the only one – "Please watch out – there are so many holes in the stage because of the appearance of scenery", you see. "You can fall into them, so watch out". Well watch out I did – mainly I watched the conductor and I made no mistake and so then they gave me the beginner's contract after that. That was the condition whether I was good enough, you see.

AS: *… at the beginning of her formal vocal training, but once that had been overcome, and she found the right person to guide her, it was plain sailing as she saw it. With Walter Legge …*

ES: It was never plain sailing. Never ever, that is really quite silly. Only then don't forget the alarms and the bombing and I had no car, I had to go by underground every time to the opera, which meant to go from our station into the town for the whatever it was called station, where you change trains again to the north west to the opera house, and that I had to do twice a day, surely. We had a car very late but that was confiscated the first day of the war and I had had it only for three months, you see. Oh yes. And you couldn't bicycle in the war through all the glass from the windows having been bombed in the war years.

AS: *… with Walter Legge, whom she was to marry, Schwarzkopf's style and technique underwent further changes. Opinions differ about Legge's effect on her singing; but his influence over Schwarzkopf between 1945 and 1964, over and above his vocal coaching, should not be underestimated.*

ES: That is all silly. It was not vocal coaching at all. He had nothing to do with vocal coaching. He never pretended to be a vocal teacher. He gave me quite different ideas, and everyone knows that. He did to everybody, not just to singers, to conductors too, violinists, too, to mezzo-sopranos, to all kinds of people, got their musical ideas from him, not the technique, for Christ's sake. That is a silly idea. And Walter would not have been so silly as to try that, you see. The only thing he ever said was, "I can hear your sound coming the right way when you do your *Schnute*", and there is a photo of me in New York and he says, "Yes, that is the sound". And that is what I ask my young singers to do.

AS: *He could be compared to an efficient engineer, with superb equipment at his disposal. It was to be he who ...*

ES: No! It is all silly. He was at heart a very big musician and not only that, he had the fantasy of all them together. You should have seen the surprised face of Flagstad, for instance, when she sang in the Number One Studio [at Abbey Road, London] and he went inside and, "Allow me Madame, but you – really, please, there should be some more expression, can you do that?" And he explained to her what he wanted – and she was sort of shhh, you know, what does this young man dare? Later she liked very much with this because she had not been talked to by somebody saying, "Now, look here, you can do that better", not singing-wise, expression-wise.

AS: *It was to be he who fine-tuned the precision instrument that was her voice and effected its smooth running.*

ES: No, that is all silly. He had no idea about technique – he had idea about sound and he asked me, "Do that sound please, Elisabeth, it needs another sound. How you do it, I don't know, but do it. Make your brain work, your fantasy work, your sound imagination". The word imagination was the key word for everything Walter did. The orchestra, the soloists, everybody. Imagination, that was the most used word. In every studio where he was listening. Oh God, I don't think I can stand it, you know.

AS: Well, shall I go on?

ES: Ja, sorry! [laughs]

AS: *Schwarzkopf's first professor of singing, though unsatisfactory, had already fostered her love of Lieder singing. At the same time, as a naturally gifted actress, Schwarzkopf knew how to project what was not a particularly large instrument to make it sound more than adequate in the opera house.*

ES: I am very pleased he knows that because I have said it hundreds of times, that my voice was not particularly loud – he doesn't have to do that because I know it full well and everybody else knows it and I have not held that back, that knowledge, you see. Ach!

AS: *History will never dub her solely a Lieder singer, because her operatic performances were gems of their own kind, planned and executed with consummate skill. Apart from Walter Legge's support, including the resource of the Philharmonia Orchestra and his influential position at EMI, Schwarzkopf relied on Herbert von Karajan at first to give her encouragement and later on a great deal …*

ES: He must not forget that many conductors who were not with EMI or were not with Columbia – they asked for me, not because they wanted to be engaged by Mr Legge, but they did ask for me, including Furtwängler and De Sabata and Cantelli, so there you are.

AS: *… a great deal of work in Vienna and Milan during the mid 1950s when he often seemed to be making unilateral decisions.*

ES: What does that mean? Who was doing that?

AS: Karajan.

ES: Karajan was what?

AS: *Schwarzkopf relied on Herbert von Karajan at first to give her encouragement and later on a great deal of work in Vienna and Milan during the mid 1950s when he often seemed to be making unilateral decisions.*

ES: What does that mean? Unilateral – what is it?

AS: It means he was making decisions by himself.

ES: But he did make decisions by himself, surely Karajan did, yes.

AS*: Whether they were the right ones or not, they all contributed to her fame and moved her to the top of her profession.*

ES: Well I agree to that, because he made me sing *Fidelio* in five concerts – was it four or five, Lily, concert performances in Switzerland?

LR: Five in five days.

ES: In five days. *Fidelio*, which I never sang. And I did agree and Walter said, "Well, with Karajan you shall be able, although the orchestra was with me on the platform and not in the pit, with your technique you will be able to do it". And Karajan wanted to frankly show a role for Leonora where you should hear that the person was vulnerable, that it was at the end of her tether, the end of her forces that she could do. That he wanted to show, never mind whether I ruined myself or not. But Walter said, "You are not ruining yourself – your technique will do it". Whether that was the right *Fidelio* I don't know but there is a conductor nowadays, Harnoncourt, who has done his *Fidelio* after that fashion. He had heard it and said, "Oh, that's it, it has to be a vulnerable voice where it comes out that she is not a heroine, she is not heroic person". A feeble voice is surely too feeble for Leonora but it was that idea and it worked and it didn't ruin me, thank God – it might have and Walter agreed, to my astonishment. Afterwards, I must say I am still astonished, but he was right, I didn't ruin myself.

AS: *There are more than passing affinities in terms of character and career between Schwarzkopf and Karajan.*

ES: Oh no, I don't think so. No, I refuse. That I do refuse.

AS: *They both suffered irritating delays after the war, when they were still …*

ES: Well, not much, for God's sake. It was mainly my illness you see, and then it was the time when I had to go through the denazification, sure, but that wasn't long. How long was it, Lily? When did I sing again after the … in '45. When did I start singing again after I was forbidden? That was *Barbiere di Siviglia* in the first operas that I was singing again in the Theater an der Wien?

ES: '45, yes I think so.

ES: '45. Yes, it was not long, perhaps a month, two months or so. We can look it up, we can see the dates – we have the dates, surely from Vienna.

LR: It was …

ES: Yes, we can say exactly how many months it was delayed through …not being through the four Allied forces of the denazification.

LR: It was not '46, anyway.

ES: No, no, it must have been the end of '45. We can see the performances, we have them.

AS: *… still politically suspect and the wheels of authority ground exceedingly slowly. Through a mixture of patience and determination they both overcame the obstacles, thanks …*

ES: By the way, I was a German citizen still and my passport and that of my mother were taken away. We were people without passports – can you imagine that then? Not now, then, and this political suspect I do refuse because everybody had to go through the denazification. But *everybody*, so there you are.

AS: *… thanks partly to Walter Legge. He had the wherewithal to accommodate them both in difficult times and to launch them as part of his grand musical plan, turning a blind eye to what some considered to be a misguidedly unpatriotic approach.*

ES: What's that? Why? Walter, an unpatriotic approach? What does it mean? That he didn't take immediately an English conductor? For thinking Karajan would be his ideal young man to eventually train his own orchestra?

AS: *His presence in both their lives immediately after the end of the war cannot be over-emphasised and was effectively the springboard from which these two artists emerged as world-famous stars.*

ES: That's true.

AS: *In the 1950s and early 1960s the leading international sopranos, apart from the special category of the Wagnerians, were Maria Callas and Elisabeth Schwarzkopf, so different ...*

ES: Oh no, no, no. Because there was still Tebaldi, also you know, for instance ...

AS: Los Angeles?

ES: Los Angeles of course, you see, sure.

AS: *... in every way that there could be no rivalry between them. Schwarzkopf was never one to make public scenes, to court the press or to walk out; she was totally professional, going about her job undemonstratively and producing a superbly finished product. This resulted in a far longer career than that of the tragic American-Greek diva, who burned herself out far too soon.*

ES: He doesn't know about it, what happened. He shouldn't imagine, because none of them knows – they should be silent about that, you see. Besides, they are now writing about a poor woman who cannot take sense to what they say, and it is really a scandal of all time. Besides, what has it got to do with her singing? Nothing. And you know not even her deterioration had to do with her private life. Oh no. She had for two years suffered from – what do you call it? Sinusitis, yes. It wasn't detected and so she sang against all this being filled up and she wanted to find the resonances which were not possible to find because those things were filled with pus. And Walter took her to [Dr] Griffiths and that's when he said he sat there holding her hand and he said, "Maria, don't be frightened – after all, you are a Greek". And she said, "Yes, but I am a frightened little Greek", you see.

AS: *... the tragic American-Greek diva, who burned herself out far too soon.*

ES: What does he know about this, the silly clot?

AS: *When Callas, in her decline, was once asked "Why don't you take up Lieder singing?", she replied, "Because I don't know any Lieder".*

ES: Yes, that's true. It wouldn't have gone with her. Her German wouldn't have been good enough. It was a different approach to singing, totally different in style, surely. It would have been a totally alien style to her, yes.

AS: *An outstanding Lieder singer has a distinct advantage over the opera or oratorio singer in that the whole focus of attention is upon her throughout the recital.*

ES: That is not always an advantage!

AS: There is no orchestra, no one to share the event and support her .

ES: Oh, the *Klugscheißer*. Everybody knows that. Silly to say those things ... oh, gosh, no!

AS: *...no scenery, no resting while others take over. There is only the accompanist, in Schwarzkopf's case Gerald Moore or Geoffrey Parsons* – and a few others of course.

ES: Oh, very many others, I wouldn't like not to mention Sawallisch, who did the first Wolf recital he was in London with me in the Festival Hall. Then there was Hermann Reutter – he did the first recital at all – did he? Or one of the early ones. Oh, there were, apart from London, there were very big ones outside. In Vienna there were different ones, in Salzburg different ones, in America different ones; in Scandinavia there were different people, of course – Levin and Olsen, and so on, yes, I had in every country the particular first accompanist of every country. Sure, in Holland, what were the names?

LR: Felix de Nobel.

ES: Felix de Nobel, yes.

AS: There were so many.

ES: Oh yes, there were a lot, but Walter really chose them from the capability of accompanying Wolf, otherwise he wouldn't have them. There was also Isepp in America, Martin Isepp, sure, he played a lot for me, and Favoretto for Lieder singing in Italy single-handedly – Giorgio Favoretto. And if you mention people, you must mention those, because it wasn't only London. It was much more difficult to sing Wolf in Rome, for that matter.

AS: *... both brilliant at their job, but none the less in her shadow.*

ES: The shadow – what was that thing?

AS: *... Gerald Moore or Geoffrey Parsons, both brilliant at their job, but none the less in her shadow.*

ES: Oh no! That is all silly. Because they all said to me afterwards, why *do* you thank them after every song you do – you turn round to thank them for their marvellous playing. I was the first one really to let them take all the time, x times through a recital, and some people said, "Oh dear, she is always turning to the pianist", you see. Yes.

AS: *It is at her Lieder recitals that Schwarzkopf scored her greatest triumphs.*
It is to be regretted that she did not have greater opportunities on stage to display more fully, and in a wider range of stage characterisations, her sense of humour, more characteristically Viennese or English than Prussian. Fiordiligi and Alice Ford were her principal vehicles for comedy, though in rather different veins, and there is much evidence of her humour in the four Johann Strauss operetta recordings as well as in the Lieder which she used to end her recitals or give as encores, like Wolf's Mausfallensprüchlein, Ich hab' in Penna *or Richard Strauss's* Hat Gesagt … bleibs nicht dabei. *She was born a German, became a British subject by marriage, was granted honorary Austrian citizenship and was then admitted to the British establishment by being dubbed the equivalent of a knighthood. Through all these cross-border travels her innate sense of fun and sparkle is unchanged.*

ES: Well, not after his book is out, you know. It is now becoming very Prussian, my humour – my good humour! It is no longer Viennese, oh no, I couldn't do it with charm, now to say something endearing, you see. Oh no, it is so upside down, all of it. I don't know anything written about me, even in the compliments, upside down and plain silly, the compliments are silly, to say the least.

AS: Well, they are backhanded, aren't they? It is almost as if he is wanting to try to find something nice to say in order to justify the horrid things.

ES: Yes – so that one can say, "Look here, after all I've said marvellous things about you".

AS: And I think she is such a wonderful singer and I've always admired her art.

ES: Yes, yes, yes.

CHAPTER ONE

AS: So now we come on to Chapter One.

ES: What is that about?

AS: *CHAPTER ONE. Upbringing in the Weimar Republic. The Third Reich. 1915-1938.*
   Olga Maria Elisabeth Frederike Schwarzkopf ...

ES: Why? Again. What have I got to do with the Weimar Republic, can you tell me that? I was the daughter of a schoolman. He can say from 1920 or whatever it is. I haven't got anything to do with the Weimar Republic, it was up in ... after the world war.

AS: What you will see in this is that he draws a parallel between your background and upbringing and German political changes.

ES: But I don't have anything to do with that.

AS: But he seeks to make ...

ES: But that is what I refuse. It is absolutely heartbreaking. Although my father was a history teacher, we never ever, ever, ever discussed anything, history or anything political – never. The only book akin to history was a German very famous, very thick *Roman* by Gustav Freytag – it was called *Die Ahnen*, "The Ancestors", and I loved it dearly and then I really went to sleep with that, wonderful. I tried to get it from here but I can't get it any more, and that was my introduction into history. Nothing, I never read a history book, shamefully I say it, because my father's subject it was. Nevertheless, I didn't. You could have asked me who was the president of whatever it was, the First Reich or the something – what is the First Reich anyway?

AS: No idea!

ES: And what was the Third Reich? That's Hitler. And what would be the Second Reich?

AS: I don't know.

ES: Surely you ought to know.

33

AS: Should I? I only know what the Third Reich was, not the First or the Second.

ES: I refuse all that, even the title. I refuse because it has nothing to do with me, whatsoever. He should state the years, from 1920 blah blah blah and that would be all, without saying anything about Republic or this one and that one, blah blah blah – it has nothing to do with me at all. I did my school years, I did my lower school, then my middle school, then I went to the Studio in Amstatt – the last one was a Studio in Amstatt where I made the *Abitur* where I only was for four months because we went only in November '33 quickly to Berlin and I had from *Dezember, Januar, Februar, März* and I must have made my *Abitur* in March and immediately I went singing, auditioning – that is where I did sing an audition – for the Music Hochschule and that's where they accepted me. Now, OK. On we go. Oh dear, I don't think I will get through that.

AS: *Olga Maria Elisabeth Frederike Schwarzkopf was born on 9 December 1915.*

ES: Moment – may I have a look? What is it called here? Where is it now? Olga, Maria, Elisabeth, Frederike – yes that's right. Unfortunately he's right there. He must have had a passport of mine – how can he know? Nobody ever knows those names.

AS: Isn't there a registry of births and deaths at your birthplace? Would it not have been registered, your birth, at some …?

ES: Where?

AS: Some local authority or something.

ES: What do you mean by local authority?

AS: Well, in England there is a registrar of births and deaths, so details are kept – they used to be in Somerset House in London – don't know where it is now.

ES: Well, we were married in, what is it called, where Ernest Newman lived – what was it called? Epsom.

AS: *Her birthplace is given correctly in reference books as Jarocin …*

ES: Jarotschin – it could be written now with a 'c' in the middle; it used to be written, when it was Germany with "tsch" in the middle.

AS: *… near Poznan, Poland; …*

ES: It wasn't Poznan then, it was Jarotschin then and Posen then, and he should be writing it with the names of then, when I was born.

AS: Well, he does go into that slightly ... *but both her parents and all four of her grandparents were Prussian.*

ES: Yes.

AS: *In 1871, Otto von Bismarck was instrumental in winning the Franco-Prussian War, and one result of the general slicing up of Poland was the return of former Prussian lands. Northern Silesia and Posen in the Prussian region were now renamed and administered by and for Germans, with former unpronounceable Polish cities and towns given German names.*

ES: I think, since I know no history, I think those things were done by the King of Saxony; I believe it was in the eighteenth century, or the beginning of the eighteenth century, when many German craftsmen were re-planted into Poland which was under his reign – or that's what they told me – in order to make the not handicraft-minded Polish poor peasants doing something in between the feudal people and the very, very poor peasants – there was no middle class; middle crafts were not there, you see, and you will find that the great churches are all built by German architects and artists.

AS: *Opportunities soon arose for Prussian citizens, especially those in the professional classes, to resettle themselves and make a good living in Posen, on the border with Russia. Friedrich Schwarzkopf, a classics schoolmaster, went to work there, even though it meant that he might have to move to a different school in a different town every three years or so; ...*

ES: He did go to work there. He was a schoolboy there and he grew up there. He started his studies in Poznan and then he went studying in Grazbad University which is now – it was Germany of course and in Munich University where he studied even under the father of Furtwängler of course – yes, true! – for Greek history. He wanted so much to become an archaeologist but they hadn't got the money for that, you see, so ...

AS: *... his methods and abilities were apparently held in high esteem. He and his young wife Elisabeth (née Fröhling) ...*

LR: Fröhlich, she was.

ES: Fröhlich, *ja,* Fröhlich she was. A very Jewish name, but she wasn't Jewish. But she grew up with the daughters of the Rabbi next door, you know.

AS: *... were living in Jarocin, near Poznan in the north of Posen, ...*

ES: I'd like to know what it is written about now – we have a Polish card – I've got that book of my cousin, that red-bound thing – where is it? I think I put it there – which he gave me for my birthday and he has got even a thing ...

LR: Somebody with a …

ES: No, it was with my name on top, in dark red cloth it is bound. And a marvellous piece of work on my life. Where did I put it? Oh dear, I had it the other day. Ah, I have it, just a minute, I'm doing the family tree back to God knows what … Liegnitz … Breslau … there's the order … and somewhere there is … oh dear, wrong glasses. Never mind … Waldsee … Somewhere here – now here it is, Posen, Poznan – and the papers of yesterday and today. It is a marvellous piece of work he did. Can I get my reading glasses, the pink ones? Now, where is Jarotschin? … Oh I have relatives all over the place there – they are mainly peasants. Cherow, that's where my father was born … Schwarzenau – there all were relatives all over the place … Gniesen – all German cities. Where is Jarotschin, we can't find it, the famous place where the Schwarzkopf … oh, when I went there – I had a concert there; the school people, children had to sing to me – it was the middle of winter, 23 degrees below.

LR: Are they [the glasses] upstairs?

ES: *Vielleicht in meine Handtasche.* Ah, here perhaps, yes here we are – I had forgotten about it.

LR: You want more coffee?

ES: No thank you, that was enough. Jarotschin … I've got family … Here's the old homestead – wait, wait, I want to find it – it gives me a bit of respite from reacting to this, you see – where is? – they take great pains to change those German names into Polish ones afterwards, Sastheim, Louisenheim, it's all very German, but you mustn't say that now, that would again be a crime, would it not? Because it was given away, it was re- … Silesia was with Polish people into there so there were no German-born people left – they were not allowed to … Jarotschin, here it is, my father born here and in Cherow, and Jarotschin was the place of my mother. It was founded in 1257 – would you believe it? Well, there you are. So, Posen … What is that here? … Liegnitz – that's where I first went to school and there's Wahlstatt – he put the yellow thing on it – where I had those four years in the boys' school – it was a Benedictine cloister, wonderful, with a marvellous Catholic church – but it was a Protestant church of the eleventh century also and then it became a *Kadettenanstalt*, where the young soldiers were trained in an *Internat* and one of them was Hindenburg … yes, trained there in Wahlstatt, and that is where the pupils were living – an *Internat*, a boarding school, but the teachers lived outside the boarding thing, but my father was there for four years – the longest we were anywhere. And that's where we all had to travel to Liegnitz for my *clavier* studies, you see. Later he went to Breslau, he had his one of his first jobs. I don't know where he was when we came out of Poland. We lived in a Bauern, a big farm, when he must have had a job already.

AS: Was he born in that area?

ES: No, we were expatriated through the French – they had trains organised to expatriate people from Poland – from Jarotschin and Poznan, if they wanted to move into Germany after the war. My father has written something very, very sweet about it, when I wasn't allowed to go with my mother out in the first trains and then he managed to get some of the French officers to have another train, the next train, again to collect me from my grandmother ... it is somewhere to be seen. My mother came from Jarotschin, where I come from also.

AS: Were they professional people, academic people?

ES: No, my mother, not at all. My father and his brother were the first academics. His brother studied – doctor for animals – what are the called? A vet, but he died quite soon after the first world war and the other two sisters, they were musical and studied music. They were very musical and had very good voices, all of them. And my mother and her sister, they grew up with her mother – her husband had died when they were sort of twelve-ish or so, or even younger, so the mother had to bring them up alone. That grandmother, where is she – *meine Oma*? My grandmother must have been a very courageous and astute woman. She lived by lending money to people who wanted money. She had only that little house and next to nothing and I've got a book there of hers with the sums that were owed her. And the girls grew up opposite the Rabbi's house and they were friends with the Rabbi's daughters and my mother learned a lot from them – for instance that the Jews teach you, immediately, that if you have been asked something – a question that you don't want to answer, you ask them a question back first – never answer, ask them back. Make something where they have to answer. She did it, all the time. Those Jews obviously had incredibly tight family connections. And what were they called? – a goy – a person who was not Jewish. The goys were not allowed into the family at all – it was a great crime for a Jewish girl to marry a goy. So she said, "Never answer – answer with a question". "How do you mean that? Can you explain? Or, did I hear right? Do you think that is the right word I understood?". No, I didn't follow it, unfortunately – I should have ...'42 – that was my first, must have done my first Susanna there. What was I looking for? Oh, the Rohmers yes, the family, that was the family of them, and that was ... we are now Poland, see, even after the first war. The things they got from German papers and he put it all together. He did that privately. Can one do that with a book, now, to have this nice printing, by what?

AS: Did he have several copies made, or just the one?

ES: No, I think just ... *they* will have one, surely, you see. "For Elisabeth, 1995". Quite wonderful. [To Lily] Have you seen it? Have you been through it?

LR: I have looked through it.

ES: Well, there you are. So, oh dear, now what – back to this – oh my!

AS: Can you tell me how you spell your mother's maiden name?

ES: FRO – with dots on – HLICH. And if I was very enough English I could say there you could see my Jewish origin because it is a very Jewish name in Germany. The first thing you would guess – aha Jewish! The names which portray something beautiful like brilliant or diament or goldstein or lustig or fröhlich, all this, yes.

AS: *He and his young wife Elisabeth (née Fröhling) were living in Jarocin, near Poznan in the north of Posen....*

ES: But that isn't in the north of Posen – I think that was in the south of Posen. I'll have to look it up. Hold it, hold it. I just had it before somewhere here – wait a minute, I can't swear to it – Jesus and Mary, where is it? Wrong glasses again. No, we are in the south-east of Posen. But that won't win our case.

AS: No, but it shows …

ES: It shows his inaccuracies, yes.

AS: *… in the north of Posen, when a royal assassination in Sarajevo turned Europe upside-down in August 1914.*
In keeping with the rise in birth-rate that the war promoted, the Schwarzkopfs soon became the parents of another Elisabeth.

ES: Oh what a silly thing. They had been seven years betrothed and my father at the moment, they surely wanted a child but it was not the rising birth rate … silly, you know.

AS: *In several respects, mother and daughter were to become much alike. There was the same distinguishing gap between the front teeth, the same shape of face and expression, the same strong-mindedness and determination.*

Frau Schwarzkopf was the forceful member of the household, which was usually the way in Germany, and especially as Dr Friedrich …

ES: He wasn't Doctor – he had not made his doctorate. No, no.

AS: *… was a kind, easy-going intellectual who liked the peaceful life.*

ES: He was a humanist, my dear. He was the ideal, humanistic person to live, if you ask anybody who met him. He lived really as a humanist – and he was also a member of – a Mason. And they also have this kind of humanistic life; he was optimist as a character, even being exposed to the most terrible things in the four years war, or more and the Russian war thing, and having to live a life to the end being an optimist.

AS: *He adored his daughter and saw to it that she was brought up in conventional middle-class surroundings, where the stated form of worship was Evangelical, …*

ES: How could he see to that? – we were in middle-class surroundings – we had no choice. I grew up where I grew up. If we had been a peasant I would have grown up there. Saw to it? That's quite silly – he didn't he see to it. We had no choice. We were a middle-class family – that was it.

AS: *… music and the arts were important, and material comfort was taken for granted, …*

ES: No, music and the arts in the beginning were not there. We had salvaged an old piano from my mother – how we did that – we must have been allowed, or he must have been allowed, to send some furniture from Jarotschin even in to

Silesia. I still don't know how that could be done, but they must have done it. Because it was the old piano, the upright, which was through the fire of the house which burned down and the water being on it but we still had it, into Berlin you know. But we didn't have a gramophone, and there was no radio, of course there wasn't. There were no concerts. In the school, in that Wahlstatt school, there were marvellous performances we did, little operas and concerts and composed things of the music teacher himself and all kinds of marvellous things and I played instruments in the marching band of the boys – I played the glockenspiel – so there. But it wasn't in the family music – oh no. He played the guitar quite well; I sang folk songs with him playing the guitar. Oh, yes.

AS: … *material comfort was taken for granted,* …

ES: What was the material comfort taken for granted? It wasn't. What do they think? There was none. There was poverty and poverty and scraping. There was really nothing.

AS: In your family?

ES: Sure – what could you have after the war? Being expatriated from one country, living in the presence of whatever it was, you know, and then going … It is all rubbish. I do remember that they scraped like hell and if my grandmother hadn't had some little saved money it wouldn't have been – she always said no, you do this for my uses here and my father went to my grandmother all the time – please help. Poverty it was.

AS: … *even during the rigours of the first world war and the depression that followed it. In career matters, Frau Schwarzkopf took charge.*

ES: The word career I refuse, anyway. There was no career to be even thought about.

AS: Now we get to all the historical stuff here – do you want to go with it?

ES: Oh dear, shall I read it in bed tonight alone? Then tell you what I think of it? What is it about?

AS: It is about the first world war and so on. Let me skip through it and see what you think.

AS: *In the summer of 1918, Emperor Wilhelm II left Berlin for neutral Holland, and Germany was forced to surrender to the Allies. A large proportion of Germans were convinced that there had been a stab in the back from within, and the whole nation, especially the Army and Navy, believed they had been cheated. It was no wonder that various political parties, including extreme right-wing factions and an ever-growing number of Communists, felt that this was the moment to oppose central control of the old kind.*
   Numerous indignities were forced upon Germany by the vengeful Allies ...

ES: But who wants to read of history in a book about me? Can you tell me that?

AS: I tell you why, because he seeks to draw a parallel between your background and German history.

ES: That I cannot understand. There are different books that you can read up on German history, there are famous books about it, but surely not that conglomeration.

AS: *... who took all her colonies and shared them out ...*

ES: You do want to hear that from a learned historian, don't you, and not from someone who writes normally on whatever, singers and so on. It is so pretentious, I can't tell you. [laughs] I'm sorry.

AS: *... among themselves, demanding 132,000 million gold marks to be paid in reparation by 1988. Everything possible was done, in fact, to ensure that Germany was prevented from waging war again in the twentieth century.*

ES: What is he talking about?

AS: I don't know. *Northern Silesia, which had belonged to Prussia for the last 200 years, and Posen, which had been Prussian for nearly as long, were both returned to Poland. While these conditions doubtless affected the Schwarzkopf family in one way or another, they had become so accustomed to Posen, and Dr Friedrich was so firmly established there, that they stayed put.*

41

ES: No, but we didn't! We left immediately after the war was finished – we were expatriated and then my father followed. He started his professional … he had to finish his studies I think very late after the … he hadn't even finished his studies – he started in the lowest languages. It was at the Provinzielle Schule Collegium in Liegnitz – where they had a branch … it was in Breslau, but in Liegnitz was a branch of it – that is where he started. Then he went to Breslau to the Provinzielle Schule Collegium. In Liegnitz I started my schooling when I was seven – there is a picture of me with the tutor there and then we went to Breslau and he was also in some other rank, I don't know what that might have been, assessor, perhaps, and then to the *Studienrat* [teacher] and from there he was then transferred to Wahlstatt where he became a *Studienrat* and he taught as a teacher of Latin, History – Greek wasn't in the curriculum – and sports, for four years, and then, after that, he was transferred again to the Provinzielle Schule Collegium in Magdeburg and then he was transferred in the year '32 to Cottbus, as the director of the school in Cottbus.

AS: *The creation and unsteady progress of the Weimar Republic was an unhappy and unruly epoch following the Emperor's abdication, for Prussia had always had a King or Kaiser since the Hohenzollerns came to power in 1701. There was an immediate and frightening devaluation of the mark …*

ES: Oh yes, that was where my grandmother, who had a piece of land still in Poland, and she could get the money of that out, had to sell it on the spur of the moment and got the money to buy a piece of black velvet – that was what her whole land was worth. And that was my concert garment, my first one, that came, hand-made by her.

AS: *… which escalated daily; strikes followed, then an unprecedented mutiny in the Navy, and growing street violence from the Communists. The young Elisabeth Schwarzkopf grew up in an atmosphere of uncertainty and change.*

ES: Oh no, not at all, I didn't know about it. I grew up in very safe surroundings, learning and things – we had the most marvellous learning facilities. We made handworks, we learned how to make baskets, we made our own masks for a very modern opera – what was it called? The *Chinesiche Nachtigall*. We made everything ourselves. We had dancing lessons, they built a *Seglerflug* [glider] and Hindenburg came to inaugurate the *Seglerflug* in the name of Hindenburg and I had to congratulate them all in front of them all – ah yes. It was the safest thing possible.

AS: So you must have been aware the mark had been devalued?

ES: I never enquired about all those things and my parents didn't see I was told.

AS: They wouldn't have passed it on to you?

ES: No, and I didn't even get *Taschengeld* – pocket money. It wasn't done. If you wanted something – well I can't remember asking for any money or anything. There was no opportunity to go out or do anything at all, in the village. It wasn't done. There was no pocket money. There was also nothing one didn't have – we had to eat. We had a little garden and that was full with eating stuff. There were cinemas in the evening in the village *Gasthof* – the first cinemas I saw, and one of them, oh, it was something with Anna May Wong, the Chinese girl whom I drew endlessly and the next one was something called Friedrich der Grossen and Katte about the friendship of the two and I drew them in all those uniforms and Friedrich der Grossen and the girls and I was smitten by that and that was the two films I saw – ever – in my youth. And then we had a market there and when the big market came, whenever that was, and on the wall of the *Gasthof* they had somebody who put up a cloth which was put into various quadrangles and one of those organs with a monkey on top and he recounted a story – one of those storytellers with music and sound – that's number one, that's number two – that's how it went. I can see that in front of me. That was our entertainment.

AS: *She had known little else, but for those of her parents' age life must have seemed uncomfortable and unpleasant.*

ES: I think it must have, but they never said that ever. They never complained to me about it.

AS: *With inflation still rampant and worsening shortages of life's necessities, there was a pressing need for a new leader to inspire the German people and get the country back on its feet.*

ES: But what has that got to do with me? Can you tell me?

AS: Well, that's what he does.

AS: *Then, as in the next post-war phase of 1945, the 'unjust' war accusation rankled deeply, because the majority of Germans considered themselves to be entirely innocent.*

ES: And why shouldn't they? Can you tell me? I wouldn't know, I wasn't told. It offends me now that he would judge the German attitude. What does he know about it? Where does he take the right to speak about Germans considering themselves what? Where does he have the right to? He is not a learned historian is he? Well, there you are.

AS: *In September 1923, when Elisabeth Schwarzkopf was not quite eight years old, the celebrated first world war strategist, General Ludendorff, lent his support to an Austrian ex-corporal and rabble-rouser called Adolf Hitler who, as head of the Deutsche Arbeiter Partei (DAP), had been campaigning for the working man since 1919. Hitler operated from Munich where he enjoyed a fair degree of support, and it was here that his Putsch took place in an effort to seize power in Bavaria. It failed, Ludendorff was discredited and Hitler was imprisoned. He would not forget those of his followers who had stood beside him in Munich, "the old Nazis", later rewarding them accordingly.*

A Schwarzkopf family photograph taken at about this time shows a tubby little girl happily skipping along during a walk with her father. He looks comfortably well built, ...

ES: Oh no, he just liked to eat. He was a – what do you call them? – he liked sweet things. My grandmother always had a package of chocolates in her compartment in the upper store of the house. She lived with us, you see, and it was in parchment and had a ribbon round it of parchment and after a while the parchment was still there but the chocolates were taken out from both of them. [laughs] Sure!

AS: *... the very picture of a successful educationalist. Elisabeth had no brothers or sisters but she got to know boys at school, where she was the only girl in her father's Greek and Latin classes.*

ES: Greek we didn't have. He didn't teach Greek. It wasn't at that school, it was only Latin.

AS: *There were changes of towns and of schools, which Elisabeth took in her stride, ...*

ES: By the way, there was another girl, we had a pensioner, [paying guest], a girl I have been talking to the other day. She lives in Scotland. We had her in order to get a little money – my mother had her in with me, you see, to grow up with me there. And then there was the Pastor's daughter who also came to that school. We were three girls, already.

AS: ... *keeping up her piano lessons and learning guitar, viola and organ as well, ...*

ES: What, what, what? Just a minute. Guitar I could start early on, viola I started only in the High School of Music in Berlin. I started with that, not before. Oh no. What was the other one? Organ? I played already in Wahlstatt in the school with the boys. I had long enough legs to reach down to the pedals and so I played the services in the morning – which were not by any religion, they were – I don't know, everybody was there, you see, not only Catholics, or Protestants or whatever, so I don't know, it was quite common when I played for the services. Some kind of chorales and things.

AS: ... *as if to counter a bias towards the sciences at the* Realgymnasium.

ES: What? Oh my! As if what?

AS: The music lessons ... *as if to counter a bias towards the sciences at the* Realgymnasium.

ES: I can't understand – does it mean they didn't like the sciences? Does it mean we didn't take the art lessons seriously?

AS: No, that there was a bias towards them, not against them.

ES: Oh no. My parents saw that I was talented for music, so that my mother deprived herself of everything she possibly could. She liked a cup of coffee but she didn't drink it. We went to Liegnitz on the bus; there was a very good piano teacher with a modern way of teaching – it was actually the way later made popular by Orff – this way of learning things and I learned my first piano playing a bit and then ear training and rhythm then – it was a method by which she had hand signs and she could indicate different voices with the two hands and we had to sing in every tonality given: it was quite a modern thing, actually, yes. No, the sciences, I was very good in school, I got very good notes, until the *Untertertia*, even mathematics but then they made me jump a class – I believe I jumped from *Untertertia* to *Untersekunde*, thereby losing the link between arithmetic and with geometry and arithmetic which I never ever weathered again, the French grammar I lost, and I never ever weathered that again and I lost – what else did I lose? – that was all, but it was quite enough to be ... It wasn't very wise to jump that thing, but they wanted, said you can and so there.

AS: *She was clearly devoted to music but she had to make her own because her family did not possess a gramophone.*

ES: Oh no, why should we? Did people have gramophones then? In the villages? No, I hadn't seen a gramophone. In the school – there was none, nowhere was there a gramophone.

AS: *Between 1922 and 1928 Friedrich Schwarzkopf's work meant that the family moved several times: from Liegnitz in Silesia to Breslau, then back to Liegnitz, ...*

ES: No, to Wahlstatt.

AS: *... which Schwarzkopf still refers to by its old name of Wahlstatt, ...*

ES: Oh no. It is quite outside Liegnitz. It is a village outside about 12 kilometres outside the border of Liegnitz and so you go through several villages in order to come to Liegnitz.

AS: The degree of inaccuracy – it is incredible.

ES: Yes it is. Well, he mustn't have any of those things to look them up, you see. And he cannot claim that it changed very much because it didn't, because we did go there with Margaret Pacy when she was the agency – and we had those concerts, I had a car in Breslau and we went with this car through Wahlstatt and Liegnitz and it had not changed a bit – it had not changed since the last war. It was left as it was. So. No, no, no, quite wrong.

AS: *... and finally back to Magdeburg in 1928, within easy reach of the Prussian capital.*

ES: Oh no, Magdeburg wasn't that easy. The next one was easy, Cottbus, but Magdeburg wasn't all that easy. No, on the Elbe. It was a good town; I didn't like the landscape at all – it was all flat. So there. But I was confirmed there and I saw my first *Aidas*, which I then could play by heart.

AS: *By this time, Elisabeth was already thinking in terms of music as a career, ...*

ES: I don't think so.

AS: How does he know, anyway?

ES: No, I went, like every youngster into the ... up there in the opera house, there was an opera house, and I don't think I saw anything else but *Aida*, up in the very, very loft. And there were those books of opera which contained in piano part all, everything, even the singing line, you see, so I could play that really from beginning to end, quite soon.

AS: *... was becoming proficient at the piano and, more important still had developed a naturally pretty, high voice which enabled her to take a leading part in her first opera, ...*

ES: Oh no. My first opera was the Haydn, The *Apotheker*, I played the comic figure of the Apotheker, being stuffed out and everything, singing the Apotheker's part, the man's. It was a women's school, you see, so someone had to take that comic part.

AS: *Eurydice in Gluck's* Orfeo ed Euridice, *at the Magdeburg school, ...*

ES: What? – the what?

AS: ... *which enabled her to take a leading part in her first opera, Eurydice in Gluck's* Orfeo ed Euridice, *at the Magdeburg school, ...*

ES: Oh no, nothing of the sort. No, no. It was The *Apotheker*, of Haydn and I have a photo of that. That's all wrong.

AS: ... *where she was also in demand at concerts and local amateur performances.*

ES: No, all wrong, everything wrong.

AS: *At one of the schools she attended, she played the glockenspiel in a marching orchestra.*

ES: No, that was in Silesia in Wahlstatt. Well, they were all boys and I was the girl in the marching band with them and played the glockenspiel.

AS: *In 1931, her father was transferred to Cottbus, ...*

ES: No, in 1932 – that was the same year when he accommodated the changing of the furniture and everything to Cottbus in the summer months, in the holidays, and I did the holidays in England, that's the thing. In the summer holidays I was sent with that other school which was so very modern, and, as I know now, was sponsored by the Social Democrats, which I can't help, to England, with bicycles and tents and we formed a madrigal choir and that's why we really loved it there. It was incredible how the English reacted to hearing me sing then, because I was very audible in the chorus, you see.

AS: ... *a twelfth-century city between Berlin and Dresden on the Polish border, ...*

ES: No, it is not on the Polish border. It is on the Polish border now, but not then.

AS: ... *and even closer to Berlin than Magdeburg, a mere seven railway stations away. The attractive countryside around Cottbus includes the River Spree with its lakes ...*

ES: It isn't lakes, it is *Wasserarmer* [literally, "water arms"] – what is it? It is all ... not lakes and not rivers, it is artificial ... you could row from there to there, and they had those famous boats which you could step then off from the right-hand side – they were not broader than that. You have those channels, canals in England, don't you? Canals, yes. It is a very famous region. It is called the *Welschen*, we call it the *Welschen*. There are several inclines in the German districts – the origin is *Welsch*, the clothes they wore, the language they spoke. *Die Welschen*.

AS: *... and the Spree Forest which used to border on the city itself. Frau Schwarzkopf recognised that if her daughter was to be properly trained as a musician, Berlin was the place ...*

ES: What? We were supposed to be in Cottbus, for how long my father was supposed to be there, you see, and then he was dismissed, so that was it.

AS: *... and the best institution was undoubtedly the Hochschule.*

ES: But, my dear, when my father was dismissed, we didn't know where to turn and we turned to Berlin because it was the nearest; and my Tante Greta lived in Berlin and she had this position in the thing and his sister Maria, she also lived in Berlin and we had those people and he had obviously friends from his student days who could help him what to do now, you see. That's what they did.

AS: It is totally misleading.

ES: Yes, it is, very.

AS: *She made inquiries and began to plan for the most significant part of Elisabeth's education.*

ES: Nothing of the kind. [There is a break in the tape at this point.] In reality, but if they do it it should just as well be right.

AS: You see, it implies that all things are a kind of smooth progression.

ES: Yes, yes it does. It implies the wrong thing and there was nothing further than of any kind of because I was still thinking I could be studying medicine which I later couldn't and my father stood there in that place said, "My dear child, you always thought you could choose between medicine and singing and we are mighty glad that you had that voice because you were not allowed into the university", and that's when he said the answer was in your *Abiturzeugnis,* that you wouldn't, on account of his history, be allowed to go to the fully-fledged university, the academic – which the Hochschule is not academic in that sense, you see.

AS: *At the time of their last move, to the Prussian capital itself in March 1933, ...*

ES: No, it's all wrong. In November, after he had been dismissed. It isn't March. In November '33.

AS: *... Elisabeth was 17 years of age. The Schwarzkopfs went to live at 8 Opitzstrasse in the Dahlem/Steglitz district of south-west Berlin. Elisabeth was entered for the Berlin Royal Augusta School and was at last in a favourable position to attend concerts ...*

ES: That's not true. I think it was ... I have to look that up. Augusta School ... it could be ... I don't know the name, I don't know.

AS: *... in a favourable position to attend concerts and share all the excitements of the capital city.*

ES: With what money? Could you tell me that, please?

AS: *She finished off her schooling by gaining her* Abitur *in 1934 and immediately applied for entrance to the Berlin Hochschule für Musik ...*

ES: But I made my *Abitur* then, having been to so many schools, by the skin of my teeth on music and drawing. I made it on Art and wrote a silly kind of thesis on the pianoforte.

AS: *... or, to give its full name, Die Staatliche Akademie Hochschule für Musik in Berlin.*

ES: It was not Akademisch – the Staatliche Hochschule für Musik in Berlin, it was. Not Akademisch, that's the point. It wasn't. If it was Akademisch I wouldn't have been allowed. No!

AS: *Thanks to her pure, sweet singing voice, her proficiency on the piano, her familiarity with the viola and organ and her knowledge of musical theory, her attractively outgoing personality and her mother's determined support, she was awarded a place.*

ES: It wasn't my mother's determined support. She was a housewife, as everybody else was a housewife, only she was the one who detected that I shouldn't stay with that singing teacher. She said, "My dear, I hear you doing those exercises and your voice has changed and it isn't what it ought to be. Even I, as a lay woman, can say that it is going very bad, what you are doing, I am sorry, but I have to say it – I hear it". She was very critical and everybody thought she wasn't the musical – she was, you know. And that is why I then left the teacher.

AS: And now we have another parallel drawn with the progress of the Nazis. *Political events in 1933 and 1934 offered welcome distractions for those Germans who recognised their salvation in the Führer. The leaders were highly visible, ...*

ES: And that has, again, has nothing to do with me. In Silesia I am sure that nothing of that ever ... hadn't seen any kind of uniform or anything at all – never. We didn't then have any radio or anything so I had no idea. Maybe that my parents knew something, but I didn't, no.

AS: *... their voices were inescapable ...*

49

ES: What was inescapable?

AS: *... their voices were inescapable ...*

ES: Which voices?

AS: Of the leaders.

ES: Well, we didn't hear them, for God's sake! What does he mean? On the radio or what? We didn't have any radio.

AS: *... over loudspeakers and wireless, and the meetings and emotionally powerful parades, organized with great skill, drew tears of hope, joy and devotion. When the Führer addressed the nation, or Goebbels spoke, mass hypnotism and even hysteria took over. Although afterwards it was difficult for people to recall what had been said, it sounded marvellous at the time, with its oft-repeated main theme, hope for the German nation at last, in the full-throated, joyous Sieg Heil!*

Even so, to others these events spelled a warning. The Jews had no doubts, and many Aryan Germans, in particular intellectuals and aristocrats, were anxious too, afraid of what the consequences might be under this new order. The generals were far from reassured by Hitler, whom they referred to as "the corporal". Yet the Nazi machine ran inexorably on, carrying the nation with it, and the longer the doubters remained, the more unlikely became their chance of reversing its progress.

ES: I don't understand, but never mind!

AS: Well, it is very insidious – because it's sort of involving you and your family in it all.

ES: Yes, but we didn't hear about it – we didn't have a radio in the first place, you see.

AS: *In the Easter holidays of 1934, before beginning her musical training, and with a grant from the League of National Socialist Students, Elisabeth left her parents in Berlin and took a cycling and camping holiday in England ...*

ES: Oh no, nothing of the sort.

AS: Well, you told me that was untrue.

ES: Well, it's in the book [compiled by her cousin, as referred to previously] you can read it. It was in 1932 it was, and it was out of Magdeburg. We went from Magdeburg by train into Bremerhafen and then we had a freighter to Hull and we had our bicycles with us and the things and we went cycling through England. Until down through Winchester down to the south coast and up again via ...

AS: And the trip was paid for by the …?

ES: By the – it must have been, that's what they tell me now, it must have been people from the Social Democratic Party because that school which made that trip with the youngsters of their own upper classes [upper school classes] who were supposed to learn English and at the same time could form a madrigal choir which we were then, from that school, where we sang concerts all over the place in England in the schools everywhere and they gave us tea and living thing. It was paid, obviously, as I found out yesterday, from the Social Democratic Party. So what – which obviously that school was – a leftish school. So there.

AS: *… for the main purpose of learning the language. The late Deryck Cooke remembered seeing her in his home town of Leicester where, she has since said she enjoyed her stay and acquired a good basic knowledge of English.*

ES: Yes, I stayed in a family there.

AS: *At this time groups of German students were beginning to travel abroad, often to schools, as a "goodwill gesture". Their political motives were possibly questionable, …*

ES: What does he mean by that?

AS: Well, I don't know … *but those who can recall the ebullience of these young Germans can vouch for their general good nature and friendliness. None the less, contemporary local newspapers reveal a generally anti-German attitude, showing very unflattering pictures of Hitler and Goebbels to emphasise an undercurrent of mistrust and unease felt by many people in England about what was going on across the Rhine.*

ES: Well, it's a good write, is it? Sure!

AS: *After her holiday, Elisabeth Schwarzkopf took her place at the Hochschule …*

ES: No. After that holiday I went then to join my parents in Cottbus: where they by then had moved to, you see. They moved in those summer holidays, which I used for this tour with that other school. I went straight to Cottbus, where to my parents had then moved and then I went into school there, which was a girls' high school or something – I can't remember what the school was, but there are pictures in the book.

AS: *… and settled down to serious study. The school's overall director, …*

ES: Where is he talking now about?

AS: He is talking about the Hochschule.

ES: In Berlin? But I didn't go to Berlin then, I only went after the *Abitur*.

LR: In 1934.

AS: *... politically appointed in 1933, was the once revered musicologist Professor Dr Fritz Stein who, in 1910, had discovered in Jena the manuscript score of a symphony which he optimistically attributed to Beethoven. Stein remained the school's director throughout the war: among the celebrated musicians on the staff of well over 100 were Paul Hindemith for composition and theory; Carl Flesch and Georg Kulenkampff, violin; Edwin Fischer and Max Trapp, piano.*

ES: Well, I never met any of them. They must have been leaving quite soon. We never met those big people. We met our singing teacher and we met our gymnastics teacher and we met the man who played us records of various singers who was a retired singer and that was the most frequented thing, we met the man who taught us the piano and the Bratsche Lehrer [viola teacher] and what else? That was it.

AS: *The most famous professor in the vocal faculty was Frau Lula Mysz-Gmeiner. Now in her late fifties, she had been an adored mezzo and Lieder singer since her first Berlin recital in 1900, ...*

ES: Yes, but she hooted – she was a hooter!

LR: It was in 1899 she sang her Berlin recital.

ES: With what? Where? I can't hear you, my dear.

LR: It was not in 1900, it was 1899 that her first recital was.

ES: Oh, yes, sure.

AS: *... and the occasional concerts she gave were always sold out. Lula Gmeiner had been a pupil of Etelka Gerster in Berlin, of Lilli Lehmann (at Brahms's recommendation) and also of the great singer and celebrated eccentric Raimund von zur Mühlen, in London. She had been so highly regarded by both Brahms and Hugo Wolf that, it is claimed, they accompanied her at the remarkably early age of 19 or 20 in recitals of their own Lieder.*

ES: Yes, that's quite true.

AS: *In 1933 Elisabeth Schwarzkopf had been to a Mysz-Gmeiner recital at the Berlin Philharmonie. Although she disliked the hooting tone which the celebrated voice produced, her "application of expression", according to Schwarzkopf, was the singer's most remarkable aspect ...*

ES: Yes, she sang the *Erlkönig* with [name unclear]. Yes. Incredible, yes.

Lula Mysz-Gmeiner

AS: *... by which she means Mysz-Gmeiner's ability to colour and underline the songs' innermost meaning by purely vocal (and facial) resources.*

ES: No, not facial. That's all silly. She wasn't that beautiful! Oh no.

AS: *This certainly left its mark after the concert which Schwarzkopf attended.*

ES: What does he mean, "which she means"? He doesn't know what I mean, does he. How can anybody say that?

AS: *With singing as her first subject and piano as second, ...*

ES: By the way, it was her last recital we went all to, in the Philharmonie, not even the Beethovensaal, in the Philharmonie, yes.

53

AS: *… Elisabeth was surprised and delighted to find that she had been assigned to Mysz-Gmeiner as her professor; but she was even more surprised and far less delighted when the great lady immediately became convinced that her new pupil, already vocally well equipped, …*

ES: No, I wasn't. I didn't know that this thing that was coming was wrong. I did it with full conviction that it was right. You do that when you are young, you do not doubt your teachers ever. Woe, if you do, you see. It was my mother who, after a year and a half, said, "Well, now, this can't go on", you know.

AS: *… would make another mezzo, and began training her accordingly.*

ES: Yes, I did it with great glee. I tried to the utmost to that, you see. I know I had to sing the *Erlkönig* in the first lesson.

AS: *Unless Gmeiner saw or heard in Schwarzkopf a familiar echo of her own youth, it is difficult to understand why she remained "despotic to the point of blindness" (or rather deafness) when the girl had such an entirely different voice. Fortunately this approach did not do any actual damage to her pupil's voice, a high, clear instrument with coloratura waiting to be brought out and a somewhat weak low register.*

ES: Yes.

AS: *But while Elisabeth progressed happily with piano, her vocal classes were another matter altogether.*

ES: That brings me to the point, you know, that, perhaps, the lower register or the middle was weak on account of having been forced into this lower register in those early days. That might have been the thing.

AS: *She attended them as instructed, using the free and lovely top to her voice far less than before, but feeling that it was all wrong.*

ES: No, no, I didn't feel that it was all wrong. I was absolutely not knowing what I was doing. I followed the advice and did it. And that is what you have to ask young people to do, you are not supposed to meet teachers who don't recognise what you can do. You are supposed to meet teachers who know what they are doing, but it can happen to everyone – to a great singer, it can happen that they cannot diagnose somebody else, analyse.

AS: *Mysz-Gmeiner's name and aura of artistic respectability were such that most girls would have considered themselves very fortunate to be assigned to her, but Elisabeth complained constantly to her mother …*

ES: No, my mother complained to me when I was practising: it was the other way round.

AS: ... *when she got home after singing lessons, feeling dispirited...* How does he know how you felt?

ES: He doesn't. He cannot. It is what he imagines, you see.

AS: It is just pure imagination.

ES: Imagination, yes, that's Walter's word, but that imagination you don't have to apply, no. Oh no. For earning money, yes he can do that. Surely, he would have earned a lot of money with this imagination by now, for a ripe old age, we hope. He will get his punishment somewhere, you know. Somebody will ... somewhere it will meet him in his own conscience, I am sure.

AS: ... *and worn out. At least she had to admit that when it came to interpretation and colouring of phrases, Mysz-Gmeiner could bring tears to the eyes; but often, in her lessons, the famous diva was close to bringing tears of anguish.*

ES: She wasn't a diva, she was a very great singer. Far from being a diva, she never sang the operatic repertoire and a diva is usually somebody on the operatic stage, not a Lieder singer, for Christ's sake. No!

AS: *From the beginning of the summer term in April 1934, there had been a new requirement at the Hochschule. All students were ordered to assemble between ten and one on Sundays for political lectures, ...*

ES: I don't know. Maybe he's right – how does he know that? Leave this page, I'll ask [name not clear] when he comes, about this.

AS: ... *either "In gratitude for the National Socialist Movement" or "The principles of Party leadership".* Well, presumably he means that you attended these meetings.

ES: That's why I want to hear [name not clear] whether we had meetings there. Maybe we did have meetings there. It could be that we were instructed at some point, but I don't ...

AS: But you don't remember it?

ES: No, I really don't.

AS: *This signalled an upheaval among the Jewish students and staff who saw the danger signals all too clearly.*

ES: One of them was my friend Carola Behr. Yes, she was.

AS: *A promising young Berliner on the Hochschule conducting course, who was a capable pianist, sometimes accompanied Schwarzkopf, as the more advanced students were required to do for the singers and solo instrumentalists.*

ES: Who was that?

AS: Well, we come to that. *Suddenly he disappeared. When it became known that he had a Jewish mother, his fellow-students did not discuss the matter. His name was Peter Gellhorn …*

ES: Oh, I see.

AS: *… and he managed to escape to England where he later took up a solid coaching and conducting career at Covent Garden and Glyndebourne.*

ES: I've got a very nice letter from Gellhorn. Oh yes, very.

AS: *In 1935 and now nearly 20 years of age, Schwarzkopf joined the students' association of the National Socialist Party at the Berlin Hochschule.*

ES: I wasn't nearly 20 years of age then at all. When did I make my *Abitur*, Lily? It was in Berlin in '34, and what was I then of age? Not nearly 20, I wasn't yet. OK, I was 19 and a half. But it sounds different!

LR: Was it in the Spring or after the Summer when you made your *Abitur*?

ES: Well, the Hochschule certainly started after the summer holidays. Must have, yes, sure. But I don't know, maybe the audition was in April, but I don't know. It sounds different from 20, doesn't it? Ah, sorry, do I bear it?

AS: *For one term she became a Führerin of the Nationalist Socialist German Students' Association …*

ES: That's what I really want to find out, but he says no, that's why they write those letters, it was a *man* who was that, you see. [See the appendix at the end of this book.]

AS: *… when she encouraged support from her colleagues in giving generously to the* Winterhilfe *(Winter Aid), …*

ES: Oh, no. I was forced … they sent me to … earn some and to restaurants and things to collect for the *Winterhilfe* [Winter Aid] – and there's nothing wrong with that, it's like you collect for the *Reute Kreiss* [Red Cross] – it's to help in Winter. What's wrong with that, for Christ's sake, really? And I know I went into that dancing thing opposite the Kapritz Hotel the first time I was in the dancing palace and I was frightened to death, you know – it was a thing where they had telephones on the tables and they telephoned each other, in the middle they were dancing –

well nobody naked to be seen, no, not that. But even so it was something so alien to me that I was very frightened but I still had to go through it and produce some money, you see, sure.

AS: *... one of the Party's favourite and continuing charities under the aegis of the Red Cross. Funds ostensibly ...*

ES: What, what? What is that again?

AS: *...* the Winterhilfe, *one of the Party's favourite and continuing charities under the aegis of the Red Cross. Funds ostensibly ...*

ES: That I don't know. But the Winterhilfe was a charitable thing that you had to do, like you would have to do any kind of charity thing now, you see.

AS: *Funds ostensibly went to poorer families in cold weather but, after the winter of 1941, demands for subscriptions were raised to help sustain soldiers on the Eastern Front.* Well, that was seven years later anyway. *Another responsibility of a Führerin was to keep an eye on other students, to ensure that they pulled their weight and said nothing disparaging about the Führer or the Party.*

ES: Oh, for Christ's sake!

AS: *This move was endorsed by Frau Schwarzkopf, who felt that the political climate favoured dedicated supporters of the Party, and although Schwarzkopf's father was personally opposed to her joining, he was obliged to concur with his wife's decision.*

ES: What he said to my mother all the time, "Please Lise, don't do a foot wrong, please put the flag out, please have the [word not clear] ready, please do the greeting. You bring us in the devil's kitchen, if you do not comply. Please, you know that we are observed and suspected. You have to be really do everything with the utmost conviction you can muster", and the same to me and he said, "Well go with it, OK, do it". Sure.

AS: This paragraph is one that has been taken up by newspapers and built into, you know, that you were spying on other students.

ES: No. How should I have been doing that, you know? Leave this page and I'll read it to [name unclear] you see. Ah, for Christ's sake. I am sure that I was one who – we went – it must have been about 40 girls in this factory. That I do know. Now, where is that vase, Lily? Where is it? It is in the side cupboard somewhere. The vase with the date round which I painted on the back – it is over the music room. Ah, that I know ... I thought it was not wrong, you see. I couldn't see any wrongness in making a holiday for working women. No, I didn't think that anything of that was wrong. I wish some people would do it now.

LR: Anything for the poor for political reasons in the top, then.

ES: Well, no, you know, it was us who had to go and do these things for the labouring women to give them a holiday, nothing more, that was all which was said and that was it.

LR: But they used it, at the top, for political ...

ES: Maybe, but I cannot. I am not guilty for anything the top does – oh no. I did it and it was asked of us and so we did it. So there.

AS: *Elisabeth was sometimes called upon to sing at public concerts with other Hochschule pupils, three of which were held towards the end of 1935. The first included two duets from Bach cantatas, when her fellow soloist was Carola Behr.*

ES: A friend of mine.

AS: But I thought she had left by that time?

ES: I don't know. That I don't know, she might have, I don't know whether she was at the time.

AS: But she was Jewish, you said?

ES: Yes.

AS: He doesn't say that, of course, does he?

ES: I am not sure that she was fully Jewish, she was certainly a kind of non-Aryan, that she was, you see. But I don't know. She is a niece, I believe, of that Mrs Behr, which I learnt later. I didn't even know who Schnabel was, you know.

AS: *They were performed to piano accompaniment. Then, in July, she sang third soprano in the Three German Folk Songs for Three Women's Voices by Brahms. At this concert, Lula Mysz-Gmeiner took the solo role in Schubert's* Ständchen *(the Serenade for Alto and Female Chorus), in which students from her singing class took part – ...*

ES: I think I remember that now, yes.

AS: *... Elisabeth included, no doubt. Another familiar name appears among the students at this concert, the soprano Gerda Lammers, ...*

ES: Yes, we were three girl friends, Carola Behr, me and Gerda Lammers. Quite true. And there was another girl called Annie Berlinige – a light soprano. I can ask [name unclear] about it. Gerda Lammers was later singing in London singing Elektra, a great success.

AS: ... *who was to become a famous Elektra and Marie in* Wozzeck *after the war. On 21 November 1935, Elisabeth sang Max Reger's* Vier schlichte Weisen *("Four Simple Ditties")* ...

ES: Yes.

AS: ... *to Albert Busch's piano accompaniment* ...

ES: That I don't know. What? I don't think so. Albert Busch. One of the Busch Quartet people?

AS: I wouldn't have thought so.

ES: Do we have that, Lily? Anywhere? Maybe it was another Busch – the name is very common – could be.

AS: ... *in the first of two evenings of German* Hausmusik *by Professor Hans Mahlke's chamber students.*

ES: I think he was the viola teacher.

AS: *Elisabeth, however, is clearly shown as belonging to Frau Professor Lula Mysz-Gmeiner's singing class, where she was still being taught as a mezzo.*
After putting up with Mysz-Gmeiner's eccentricities, as she saw them, for more than a year, ...

ES: I didn't see them as eccentricities at all. When my mother kept on saying it doesn't sound right, well, I still did it until it dawned that one would have to do something. But I wouldn't have called it "eccentricities". It was her method of teaching and she was wrong. She got her analysis of me wrong. That was all there was to it.

AS: ... *Schwarzkopf was at last able to convince her mother about the inadequacy of her training.*

ES: No, we talked it over and my mother then said, "What can we do, for God's sake, it had never been done that somebody left such a famous teacher, and that will be a catastrophe". Which it was.

AS: *It was now agreed that something was radically wrong, not least because of her lack of any real vocal progress.*
Frau Schwarzkopf went to see Professor Stein and vigorously presented her case to him.

ES: That may be, I don't know, I can't remember that. She may have done it, yes.

AS: *The initial reaction was indignation.*

ES: Because I would have been afraid. But I don't know it. It is new to me to hear it for the first time but maybe he has heard it from someone – who knows?

AS: *Nobody before had dreamt of turning down instruction from such a wonderful artist as Mysz-Gmeiner:*

ES: That's quite true, yes.

AS: *... it should have been an honour to sit at the Frau Professor's feet ... Thus ran Professor Stein's argument.*

ES: Yes, quite true.

AS: *But the determined Frau Schwarzkopf disagreed, and won the day. There could be no question of Elisabeth's being transferred to another professor at the Hochschule for the time being; indeed, the situation had to be tactfully negotiated to avoid causing embarrassment to Frau Professor Lula.*

ES: Yes, surely.

AS: *Yet some time, between her last concert ...*

ES: You don't say Frau Professor Lula, you always say the family name. Are you having pains? Somewhere there?

AS: I just feel a little bit – I'm OK.

ES: What is it? Cold?

AS: No, I'm just a little bit stiff, that's all.

ES: Shall we have a glass of something?

AS: That might be quite a nice idea ...

ES: Yes it might be – we there have some there kind of those Austrian whatever they are, those down there, those spirits from ... [break in the tape].

AS: *There could be no question of Elisabeth's being transferred to another professor at the Hochschule for the time being; indeed, the situation had to be tactfully negotiated to avoid causing embarrassment to Frau Professor Lula.* Then you said she would never be referred to as Frau Professor Lula.

ES: Yes.

AS: *Yet some time between her last concert in November and another one before Christmas, Elisabeth acquired a new professor, as the programme makes clear.*

ES: What, what, what? For what?

AS: For singing.

ES: Yes, but outside the Hochschule.

AS: Outside?

ES: Outside the Hochschule. Yes, I went to somebody who used to be a singer and Herr Egenolf who was a tenor.

AS: Yes, he does say that.

ES: That is outside the Hochschule of Music.

AS: *On 20 December a large body of student singers accompanied by the Chamber Orchestra of the Hochschule and conducted by Professor Dr Fritz Stein performed Heinrich Schütz's* Weihnachtshistorie *("Christmas Story") to commemorate the composer's 350th birthday. The first of the Three Shepherds was taken by Elisabeth Schwarzkopf. One of the basses on this occasion, Otto von Rohr, became a concert and opera singer of repute after the war.*

ES: Yes, he was, I believe, in the south of Germany, somewhere.

AS: *It has always been assumed that, having secured her release from Mysz-Gmeiner, Elisabeth immediately started to study with a Dr Egonolf [sic] outside the Hochschule. But on 17 June 1937 she sang Schubert's* Four Canzonets (D688) *accompanied by Professor Arthur Kusterer, to whose Lieder class, the programme states, she now belonged.*

ES: The Lieder class, that was a totally different thing, not connected with the singing teacher. They were studying Lieder, studying whatever, you know. Where do we have the name of Kusterer, Lily? In something else.

LR: One of the conductors of an opera who ...

ES: He conducted an opera in Berlin – in the opera later. He was a conductor. But nothing to do with the singing teacher.

AS: *Eventually, of course, Dr Egonolf became interested in her voice, concurred that she was no mezzo, and expressed confidence in her future as a coloratura soprano. He acknowledged the value of some of her former teaching, especially Mysz-Gmeiner's lessons in interpretation. But essentially Elisabeth was asked to submit to fresh instruction, and was only too glad to agree. From this point onwards her progress was rapid and the singing lessons went from strength to strength.*

ES: Yes, although he had a method which I didn't adopt, as yet I don't understand. I think he took the wrong expression. He wanted something of *Rand* [edge], I don't know. I think he wanted to concentrate on the whistling register of the soprano and that's what went totally wrong. Anyway, I suddenly became a very strident, silvery, as they say, soprano. But his wife was a ballet teacher. She taught us moving on the stage and that was valuable. I learned from him support, the *appogio*. That he really could get you doing. If you know how many of my young singers have no idea what is support – how should I support the *appogio*?, the *Stütze* [support], for singing, which is a technical thing. It is the first thing you ought to learn, but I never did, not even with Mysz-Gmeiner, oh no.

[LR coughs]

ES: My goodness, what is ever that? Have you taken a pill or something – to loosen it? Thank God she is far enough away from me!

LR: I didn't cough yesterday.

ES: No, but you do today.

LR: Sorry!

AS: *For some time now her sights had been set on one of the Berlin opera houses. The Deutsches Opernhaus in Charlottenburg was the most conveniently situated …*

ES: Oh no. Does he also say that I also went for half a year to the Stern'sche Konservatorium. That was even in, or after the Egenolf time, before I went to the opera house, I believe, to study, well that for half a year, it was a very famous conservatory, [she spells out] STERN'SCHE Konservatorium, ja, and there we had stage … working on different parts of the opera, you see. Me, in particular, on the Agathe aria, which I shouldn't have done at all with my light voice, but they made me work on that, and that served me, then, for the audition for the opera.

LR: He spells it Egonolf.

ES: Egenolf.

AS: *… conveniently situated and seemed to be of a high standard, less reactionary, and under a more approachable management …*

ES: What does that matter to me? It was one of the opera houses. What did I know about their standard, or about anything? It doesn't matter two hoots what he thinks it was like. It was one of the opera houses where there were auditions, whatever it was. This thing what he says about it is of no, no, *wie sagt man das*?

AS: Consequence.

ES: Yes. No, it is the first time I hear about this – balls, you know. [She laughs] Sorry, but *really*! Well, you can apply one's own opinion to everything surely, but this man wasn't even there, so what does he know what the opera house was like? Nor did we. We knew it was one of our great ... the Staatsoper was auditioning. The time for auditioning, as it is here in the Zürich Opera House, there are some days when they have 20 singers auditioning. OK. That was one of those days, there, you see.

AS: *... more approachable management than that of the proud old Staatsoper.*

ES: What was that?

AS: Well, he says that Charlottenburg was a more approachable management than ...

ES: Approachable? No, it simply happened to have auditions, at that time, and the Staatsoper didn't. So there.

AS: *With this ambition in mind, she continued to take singing lessons from Dr Egonolf.*

ES: Oh no, I hadn't this in mind at all, before to take singing lessons. I didn't have any ideas about an opera house, I simply took singing lessons and the opera house came in when suddenly someone said, "Oh, well, they have auditions, you might just as well" – that was some time before I did it, you see.

AS: *... she continued to take singing lessons from Dr Egonolf who was undoubtedly the right teacher for her. Indeed, after passing all her musical examinations with merit and graduating in 1937 ...*

LR: 1938, not 1937.

ES: Not in all respects he was the right teacher. He wasn't in all respects. That's not true. He was in some respects, as to the *appogio*, and to his wife teaching the ballet, that was fine, you see, but the other things he taught me were not good.

AS: Lily, you say Elisabeth graduated in 1938, not 1937.

ES: What did I do?

LR: Graduated in 1938, not 1937.

ES: What do you mean graduated? To what?

63

LR: From the musical examinations.

ES: Oh, you mean the *Abitur*? No, what do you mean?

LR: After the Hochschule.

ES: I didn't do any examinations, for God's sake, I didn't finish the Hochschule. I went away, you know, only stayed a few ... I never did any examinations because there were no ... I can't remember there were any examinations for young students. There were not, really, at that time, it is the first time I hear that.

LR: ... in '38.

ES: Oh, no. Wait a minute. I went to the Hochschule in '34. I sang auditioning to the Hochschule in April or March '34, immediately after my school *Abitur*, which must have been the end of March '34, and then I sang for the auditioning for the Hochschule, and was accepted out of about 50 and more singers into the class of Lula Mysz-Gmeiner, and I stayed with Mysz-Gmeiner until, I think, the end of '35, when already, or in the beginning of '36, at the latest, already came this kind of working towards the separation from ... It didn't go overnight, you know. Of course not. One had to talk it over with my family and so on, for how we are going to do that and how does one not hurt the Professor and so on and so on. Can it be done? It had never been done, as far as I know, before, so how does one go about it? That didn't occur so easily, because in '36, I believe, I was still taking part in this factory business and what was else in '36? Something else – I can't ... What was it? Oh, '36, I don't know which 1st of May it must have been, '35, '36 we all had to go to the Templehof für Welt for the 1st of May celebrations, ten thousands of whatever people at the whole high school had to go and so on. That was when previously had been a Communist or ... the Labour day, which evidently it was turned round in some ... and that was the only time I saw Hitler live, you see, from about, well, I don't know where I stood, but I saw him from afar, sure, you see. That's why it is important, because they say I knew him and God knows what and we know our Russian friend from the examinations there [in 1945], I don't have to repeat that. So, now, where are we again?

AS: *After passing all her examinations with merit and ...*

ES: I didn't pass any examinations! I left everything, you see.

AS: OK. *...graduating in 1937 ...* Lily says 1938 ... *she became a member of the Hochschule's advanced course at their Opera School.*

ES: I didn't, I went to the Stern'sche Konservatorium, as an opera school. I was not in the opera school in the Hochschule. Oh no. Besides, I don't think there was one – I can't remember.

AS: *Between November and the following April ...*

ES: I should calm down, you know, shouldn't get so excited over every little bit, you know.

AS: ... *she appeared in its production of the 1930 Brecht-Weill children's opera* Der Jasager *("The Yes-Sayer"), which seems a curious choice.*

LR: As if it was Elisabeth's choice.

AS: No, I don't read that into it. *Both Brecht and Weill had been forced to leave Germany by 1933, ...*

ES: That's why I don't think it *is* a curious choice. The man is silly. Why shouldn't we do that?

AS: ... *and in that year Weill's music was officially banned as decadent Marxist rubbish.*

ES: Maybe we did it before that, I don't know.

AS: *Nevertheless, their opera is about sacrifice for a cause, and begins with a static chorus intoning, "Above all, it is important to learn consent".*

ES: It doesn't matter two hoots what the opera was about, I just sang a role in it, obviously. I can't remember what it was about – it might have been ...

AS: It is all leading up to the same thing.

ES: Up to the same thing.

AS: *Small wonder that Brecht and Weill followed it later with* Der Neinsager.

ES: Did they?

AS: *Besides becoming a member of the Opera School, ...*

ES: I wasn't!

AS: ... *Schwarzkopf joined the Favre Solistenvereinigung ...*

ES: Yes, but that was not then, that was later.

AS: ... *a chorus of semi-professionals, music students and serious amateurs in Berlin founded by the opera singer Waldo Favre.*

ES: Yes, not only was he an opera singer, but he was a very good chorus master – a Swiss man.

AS: *They sang secular and sacred (but no Jewish) works.*

ES: How do I know? How does he know, for Christ's sake? Honestly! [laughs]

AS: *At about the time that Schwarzkopf joined, Favre had secured an engagement for them to sing the chorus in a recording of* Die Zauberflöte.

ES: Besides, you know, nowhere, in after a while, Jewish composers were … Mendelssohn wasn't played, was it? It's as if we, alone, sang no Jewish things. All those composers were no longer played. We know that and no, no, when we had the war with the English, and I still sang the madrigals translated by Herr [name not clear] into German and it was only said *madrigale* in a concert – me, as the soloist which was totally out of style, but never mind. It was a famous party piece of Ivogün, which she gave to me. And nobody knew it was English madrigals – because we were not allowed.

LR: Beecham's name was not mentioned in Denmark on the label of the German pressing of the recording of the *Zauberflöte*.

ES: Oh, really!

LR: Because he was an Englishman.

ES: I didn't know that. That is interesting.

AS: *A tight budget may have demanded the recording company's use of such a body, less expensive to engage than either the Staatsoper or the Deutsche Oper,* …

ES: But there was also another chorus, and that was the … what was it? Singemeinschaft, yes, yes.

AS: … *but well up to the task all the same.* Was it true that they engaged you because you were less expensive than the Staatsoper or the Deutsche Oper?

ES: I don't know anything about being engaged and the finances of it. I didn't know that.

AS: It seems questionable. *The recording was due to take place in the rococo Beethovensaal of the Philharmonie in Bernburgerstrasse,* …

ES: It wasn't a rococo saal at all; it was the adhering style to the smaller hall, in the Philharmonie. No way of rococo. The idiot, you know. That was built in the last century. Rococo! Does he know what rococo is? Ah Christ! [laughs]

AS: … *conducted by the celebrated and eccentric English impresario, Sir Thomas Beecham,* …

ES: What? He was not an impresario.

AS: Well, he was, in a way.

ES: But he was a conductor.

AS: He was both, actually.

ES: He wasn't known as an impresario, my dear, he was known as a conductor. Surely.

AS: Well, principally a conductor, yes.

ES: But an impresario is somebody like an agent, nowadays. Now, come on. I didn't even know that he had that kind of particular distinction, you see. That's news to me, the first time I hear it.

AS: It is a misleading description of him.

ES: Yes. It is. And unfair. If you know the opinion of Walter for impresarios!

AS: *… who brought a highly competent young man from London with him as his technical assistant. His name was Walter Legge. Schwarzkopf sang as a chorus first soprano in this famous recording, with three days of sessions in November 1937: it was an exciting experience and her first real engagement.*

ES: What, what, what?

AS: *…it was an exciting experience and her first real engagement.*

ES: Was it? My first real engagement for anything? No, it must have been in the Rundfunk and where we were before. Surely, with the chorus. Yes, sure, although it was only with the chorus, also.

AS: *Her eyes positively feasted on Tiana Lemnitz, Erna Berger and Helge Roswaenge, …*

ES: It is really rubbish, you know.

AS: *… world-famous artists who were standing singing so close to her.*

ES: Well, it is quite true that – that was an incredible thing for us to see them also so near, that is true. But who is he to say that? Oh! He knows what one wore as a dress or something? It is so – *wie sagt man da?* – so pretentious – to write that he would have known. How does he know? I might not have liked her at all, and he wouldn't know. No.

AS: *On 1 March 1939, shortly before leaving the Opera School, Schwarzkopf was admitted ...*

ES: What, what, what? Which year?

AS: *1 March 1939.*

ES: But 1939, in the Autumn, it was the beginning of the war. And in '39 I was already a member of the opera – I was engaged ... [break in the tape]

AS: *On 1 March 1939, shortly before leaving the Opera School, Schwarzkopf was admitted as a member of Dr Goebbels's Reichstheaterkammer (RTK), part of the Reich Ministry for Public Enlightenment and Propaganda (ProMi). She was given the number 67784, ...*

ES: Could well be, we all were.

AS: *... a serious step towards joining the NSDAP ...*

ES: Oh no. It was, of course a professional thing, you had to be, everybody was, immediately.

AS: *... a serious step towards joining the NSDAP and becoming what we would now describe as "streetwise".*

ES: What does that mean?

AS: Streetwise means someone who is knowing, knows the ins and outs of things. It is very sort of ...

ES: Well, that is really very mean. It is one of the meanest things, you see. Yes. Now listen. But it isn't true, because we must have been member of the *Reichsmusikkammer* the moment I was ... said – will you get a contract as a beginner, sure, and, by that same token, you were in the *Reichsmusikkammer*, a member of whatever *Kammer* whatever it was, the under thing, with the *Reischstadt* there were underlings like Schauspieler and Opera and so and so on – the overhead was the *Reichsmusikkammer*, which also Furtwängler was in, and so on, the President of, you see. So there. But it was in '38 I got my contract to start officially on the whatever, the first of September '38 – I had already been singing in the last days of summer, after my first audition and my jumping in for the Flowermaiden, *Parsifal* and immediately they put me into small roles ... you had better see all the things I sang then until my official term started in September, in '38, and '39 I was already in the opera house, as a beginner, with the title of an *Anfänger* [beginner], it was the *Anfänger* contract, a special contract for beginners – and a very good one it was, namely to sing everything they gave me, on the spur of the moment, overnight. So that's very wrong. Really very wrong, that date.

AS: So that ends chapter 1 and now we come to Chapter 2 which is "Opera Singer in Berlin 1938 to 1940".

ES: By the way. To make it quite clear to you: this *Musikkammer* was automatic. If you had an engagement in the theatre, you belonged to the appertaining chamber, the *Musikkammer*, the *Theaterkammer* or whatever the professional thing was.

AS: You see, when he says Schwarzkopf was admitted as a member of it, it suggests that you …

ES: Applied for it. No, no – it was automatic. You didn't even know – it was quite automatic and that was it, you see. You couldn't perform if you were not – it was impossible. Everybody was automatically in this same realm, you know, or whatever it was, this government thing, especially when you started this profession – it was the first thing, you see. Which you were not asked – you will not ask, it was automatic. Because it is a professional chamber, like somebody who is a lawyer and is being in the lawyers' whatever – there must be a kind of professional body immediately, when he is a lawyer. Now that was the professional body, nothing to do with the Nazi thing, at all.

AS: So it wasn't Dr Goebbels's Reichstheaterkammer, it was just …

ES: He was the Reich [word not clear] of propaganda – he was that overall, over everything, you see.

AS: So it wasn't something that had been set up by him?

ES: It may be. I don't know whether it existed before the Nazis, that I don't know. I really have no idea, because I wasn't at the theatre, so I don't know. But I don't think it existed before, but it wasn't the *Nazionalesozialistische Theaterkammer*, it was the professional chamber for a certain profession of musicians or players or whatever. We'd better look up Mr - what's his name? The one Schreiber, Schrieber, Schreiber – this one there, in the book. He should surely be writing on the *Reichstheaterkammer*, the *Reichsmusikkammer* or whatever the chambers were.

CHAPTER TWO

AS: *Chapter 2: Opera Singer in Berlin 1938-1940.*
Das Deutsche Opernhaus auf dem Bismarckstrasse ...

ES: Auf *der* Bismarckstrasse.

AS: Auf *der*?

ES: Das Opernhaus in *der* Bismarkstrasse.

AS: He says *dem*.

ES: Oh, hopeless, silly, *in der, nicht auf.*

AS: *... was the official name of the Deutsche Oper when the 22-year-old Elisabeth Schwarzkopf joined its company. On Wednesday, 13 April 1938 she attended an audition there before Wilhelm Rode, the General Intendant, Hans Batteux, ...*

ES: Batteux, a very famous *Regisseur* [director], a very good one.

AS: *... his deputy and chief producer, and Artur Rother, the newly appointed First Kapellmeister (Director of Music). Schwarzkopf sang Agathe's scene, "Wie nahte mir der Schlummer ... Leise, leise" from* Der Freischütz, *an ideal vehicle for displaying her legato at the start, and later showing off her top B.*

ES: That's all silly. It had nothing to do with *legato*, they wanted to hear the voice, and that was all, you see, and what it was anyway, because I wasn't a direct soprano then.

AS: *Egonolf [sic], who had prepared her for this audition, knew exactly what he was doing.*

ES: It must have been still Egenolf, although I was already in the *Opernschule* to learn the stagecraft for that particular part, you see. But I think I still was with Egenolf – I can't put my finger on when I left him, actually. Maybe I was still for some time.

LR: It says in his book that you were studying with him for four years.

ES: It could be, that I don't know. What kind of book is that? Of Egenolf?

71

LR: Yes.

ES: Is there? I haven't seen that.

LR: I have that book at home.

ES: Well, it could be, but I can't swear to that, you know. So there.

LR: He writes that you came in the Autumn of '36 and stayed for four years.

ES: It could be. But it depends on when I really went to Ivogün, when was that? It must have been '41, beginning. After the first Zerbinetta, of that we have the exact date. When is that? The first Zerbinetta?

LR: September '41.

ES: September '41. Well, then I must have been going, after that, maybe in October or so starting Ivogün in '41. Yes, OK.

AS: *The three executives were satisfied with Schwarzkopf's performance and told her that they were considering her for a part in a new production of* Parsifal.

ES: Oh no. They were asking me whether I could jump in – they had lost that second *Blumenmädchen*, not the next day but the Friday, on Good Friday whether I could take it over, you see. A new production – I would have had rehearsals, I didn't know what it ever was, a new production, an old production, besides they played *Parsifal* every year at Easter time, you see. But I never heard it. Ah Christ, so silly.

AS: *Her debut would be in the short but important role of Second Flower Maiden (First Group) in Act II.*

ES: But they were all important, all the Flowermaidens. Every one of them is important. It is just silly to say to say that.

LR: Here he goes against himself also, because in the list [of performances, page 229] he writes the opposite – he writes first *Blumenmädchen*, second group.

ES: Ah, I see.

AS: *This was a demanding offer to someone who had never appeared on the professional stage before, especially on an opening night.*

ES: It wasn't an opening night. It was Good Friday's performance of *Parsifal*, as there was every year. There are no opening nights for those things; it was the performance for every year in the Easter week. Ah, God, the man has no idea.

AS: *The role involves solos interspersed among other sopranos' lines, and ensembles of great precision with stage movement by the whole chorus of Flower Maidens. Such roles were sometimes offered to test the more promising young singers in Germany and Austria; …*

ES: It wasn't the normal testing opera, it was because they hadn't got one – somebody had fallen ill. You never would give a beginner a role like that, if there wasn't a dire need for it, you see.

AS: *… and although Schwarzkopf gathered that it was not an altogether unusual event, it was nevertheless a compliment to her. To the question, "Can you sing this role? Do you know it?" the plucky, ambitious girl replied, "Of course I do!"*

ES: I hate this word "ambition" coming in. I either wanted to sing or didn't want to sing. And I wasn't plucky, I was confident that I could sight-read and learn very fast, already. You see, if I wouldn't have known that – and I could learn very fast, and later on as you know from Stravinsky, even in my older years, I could learn very fast, namely the role, while I was singing in Bayern, I learnt the Stravinsky in English in a Russified English in one week. Ah, silly clot.

Arthur Rother

AS: *Of course she didn't. There was a bigger snag.*

"We are inviting you to sing it", said Rode, "but the first performance is on Good Friday, the day after tomorrow. You have only 36 hours in which to prepare – and Herr Rother will be conducting!" Sounds as if they had a tape recording – all this direct speech.

Elisabeth went straight home and devoured the score. Her mother, ever ambitious for her daughter, was delighted.

ES: Now that is really, that is the final offence, speaking about my mother in that way. Really. My mother would have been the one who, surely, would say, "Are you crazy?" – she didn't know *Parsifal*, either, but she said, "How can you do that?" and I thought, "I can", I saw the score and I can learn it the day after tomorrow, I have it. I know.

AS: *One piano rehearsal at the Opera House was followed ...*

ES: By the way, you don't learn a role like that through ambition. You learn it because you are gifted for learning, not being ambitious. Ambition doesn't help you there two bits, you know. No!

AS: *... at the Opera House was followed by a run-through of her moves on stage ...*

ES: Which wasn't. I wasn't on stage, no, at all. I went on stage and they said: "Don't fall into the proscenium" – what do you call it? In the stage, the holes, that was all. "Look to the other singers and stay with them".

AS: *... which Elisabeth picked up at once, displaying the kind of determination that is one of her characteristics. On Good Friday she arrived at the Deutsche Oper in good time for the 18.30 performance.*

ES: I wonder whether that word "determination", in the context of being extraordinarily gifted, not for a singer but as a musical person. The "determination", when you are extraordinarily musical – isn't the word, you know: I was confident that I could learn it. Sure, you know, that was not really a ... I had been singing sight-reading with the choruses all the time – sight-reading and learning those things. It was nothing, doing it, obviously. And I did it later – you ask that man Rode, he said, "I know you learnt the *Waffenschmied* overnight and then did it without a rehearsal" – which is more difficult because it is arias and things and what have you and dialogue. Dialogue is very difficult to learn because it hasn't got music attached to it. If you have music attached to words it is very much easier to learn than words alone.

AS: *She whistled Wagner's tune ...*

ES: The tune is not the thing, it is the notes. There is no tune!

AS: *... as she went up to the dressing-room which she shared with the other Flower Maidens. Whistling in the theatre means bad luck, and little allowance for the beginner was made by the other superstitious girls, ...*

ES: It was not girls, it was the great singers of the opera house. Have we got the cast of the *Parsifal*, somewhere? Sure, in the programme. It was the great singers who sang *Traviata* and all those – they were, that was the usual thing, as in Vienna and the great opera houses, it is the high sopranos, and then, of course, the lower ones for lower parts, but it is the great singers who do it. That was the thing: it wasn't just little bit singers, oh no.

AS: *... the other superstitious girls, who looked as though they wanted to scratch her eyes out! Once on stage, Schwarzkopf held Artur Rother's eyes fast with her own, and got through the ordeal safely, enjoying her proximity ...*

ES: Perhaps I did say it in some interview to somebody, because he must have got those things ...

AS: There's a reference to that somewhere. ... *the ordeal safely, enjoying her proximity to the American Wagnerian tenor, Eyvind Laholm, who was singing Parsifal.*

ES: Silly. I didn't listen to anything at all, I just got through it, and that was it, you see. Oh no. The man we did all adore as Parsifal was Gotthelf Pistor. Yes, that was the great man, Parsifal and all the other things he did. That was a revelation. The chorus, everybody stood in the wings to see him – it was such an expression of that one, not a fantastic voice, but, as an artist, incredible. Yes, Gotthelf Pistor.

AS: *On that night, of 15 April 1938, Elisabeth Schwarzkopf became a probationary junior soprano in the Deutsch Oper, Berlin, ...*

ES: What is that called – an *Anfänger*? Is that the title of a beginner? Those were the contracts – a beginner's contract, an *Anfänger Kontrakt*. That is what it was even printed upon, an *Anfänger*, beginner.

AS: *... with her name appearing on the programme and then on the artists' notice board for forthcoming operas, all of which had to be learned immediately. The first was Wellgunde in both* Das Rheingold *and* Götterdämmerung.

ES: Was it? Lily? The first part to learn after the audition? No, not at all. It wasn't. But again, it seems as if I already had the biggish roles. After all, it is quite an important thing, I thought I sang, not Wellgunde, but ...

LR: Wellgunde – 26 April.

ES: Was it? What came in between?

LR: Nothing between *Parsifal* and that concert.

ES: Really? Well, he must have had a lot of confidence. Maybe it was the same singer missing as for *Parsifal*. It could be.

Gotthelf Pistor

AS: *Five more roles followed before the end of the season in August, and now the staff repetiteurs and coaches were on hand to help her.*

ES: And what were those roles? – now you start telling me – it was the Hirtenknabe and then I think it was the First Boy in *Magic Flute*.

LR: Ida?

ES: Ida, which has two sentences to sing solo, the sister of Adele in *Fledermaus*, which I sang for all eternity, what was it after Wellgunde, immediately?

LR: Lumpensammlering.

ES: Lumpensammlering? which has four words to sing … "hader, hader, hader alle", which means – Lumpensammlering – old clothing. Does he mention those?

AS: No, he doesn't.

ES: Yes, and that's what it is. They think I sang only those things, you see.

LR: Hirtenknabe in *Tannhäuser*.

ES: The Hirtenknabe, what was it? Not the Knabe, what was it? Tannhäuser Page. Which was four pages singing, not solo at all.

LR: Esmeralda in *Verkaufte Braut*.

ES: Esmeralda in *Verkaufte Braut*, which was a little bit bigger, a little dancer girl there, that was.

LR: And then again Ida.

ES: Ida, yes, *Fledermaus*.

LR: And then Marie.

ES: That's what I took over overnight. *Waffenschmied*.

LR: And then, for a change, Ida.

AS: Well, we've got the picture.

LR: And then came Bertha, *Euryanthe*.

ES: That was something idiotic and small.

LR: In September '38.

ES: '38, yes, that is when I had already started the genuine beginner's contract, which started at the beginning of September. But he should mention those, because it looks as if I am already, what did she do, the Flower Maiden and Wellgunde – oh my God, you know, and surely I can't understand it either how they dared give it to me. Because it must have been that somebody had fallen ill.

AS: *This was a remarkable opportunity for such a young and inexperienced singer, because starting an operatic career in Germany usually meant a first engagement (if you were lucky) at one of the provincial houses of Chemnitz, Oldenburg or Stettin. But in one stride Schwarzkopf had arrived in Berlin's second opera house and attained status above that of a mere chorus member.*

ES: Yes, chorus member, yes, but I was still a beginner for two years. Oh, I say …

AS: But he doesn't say that, does he?

ES: No, he avoids that, you see.

AS: It's all deliberate.

ES: It's all deliberate, yes. This came out in the paper here, our little paper, and of course she made a comet-like career on the big opera house, she didn't go to the provinces, as was the usual thing. OK. And the next day was a concert here by Julianne Banse, a very very good young singer, I myself made to give her a prize, a Schubert prize, and she gave a recital here, then in the same paper, ours, next day, ... "of course, Julianne Banse, she is so gifted she sings even Pamina in the big opera house in Berlin in the beginner's year". They measure with two measures, you see. Me, it was, of course, she had the big status of a something star, by the way, a comet-like – but I don't call it comet-like when you have to sing the Lumpensammlerin, with four words to sing. That's not a comet-like or the thing in *Freischütz*, those girls who were the *Brautjungfer* [she sings a short phrase] which I sang for all eternity, even after my recitals I did sing it, you see. They made me sing that again – that was the moment when I had a soubrette and coloratura's contract and Ivogün said, "You don't have to, you don't have to let them in the lurch if they don't have anybody for that role at the moment. But you can ask to sing it with another name. And then I did sing it under the name of Maria Helfer, because I'd sold out the Beethovensaal, three times, first time was given away the tickets by Raucheisen and the next three times recitals in the same winter season were sold out. That was what – in '42.

AS: Then he goes into a long rigmarole about the Charlottenburg.

ES: He really is a swine, that man.

AS: Shall I go on?

ES: I don't know whether I can stand all that, you know.

AS: This is just about the opera house.

AS: *The Deutsche Oper had begun as the Charlottenburg Opera, in that western district of Berlin whose local council, funded by shareholders, had built the first private Berlin opera house.*

ES: What was that? Funded by what?

AS: Shareholders.

ES: Well, it doesn't interest me. It doesn't have anything to do with me.

AS: *It held an audience of 2,300 and opened as the Städtische (City) Opera in November 1912 with* Fidelio. *A resident company of reasonably good singers was inadequately supported by the artistic standards achieved, which neither the first world war nor the depression which followed it helped to improve. In early 1923, Otto Klemperer was invited to join the Charlottenburg as musical director so as to inject some vigour into the company, but he saw too many artistic and financial difficulties ahead and was put off by the building which was "singularly lacking in charm but large and technically up to date".*

ES: But very good acoustics, though.

AS: *So he declined the offer. On Christmas Day 1924 the Charlottenburg Opera was declared bankrupt and was immediately seized by the Greater Berlin City Council who owned the land on which the building stood. The Chief Burgomaster of Berlin had long wanted to establish an opera house with direct civic subsidy, in contrast to the established Staatsoper with its history of royal patronage, altogether at odds with the character of the present Weimar Republic.*

ES: We can leave this out.

AS: Shall I skip the next bit? I think we ought to pick it up here: *The company achieved even greater artistic successes when Carl Ebert, from the Darmstadt Opera, was appointed General Director in charge of productions in 1931.*

ES: I don't know –I didn't know that. I don't think it was in my time.

AS: *He brought with him Rudolf Bing, ...*

ES: Ha! Well, there you are.

AS: *... his astute young general manager, whose ways, because he was thoroughly Viennese, were sometimes at odds with Prussian methods. But Ebert and Bing again raised the production standards, ...*

ES: Well, that has nothing to do with me, either.

AS: *... making them in many ways preferable to those at the Staatsoper, an unheard of state of affairs:* Stadt *versus* Staat.
Unfortunately, some of the pride in achievement and good personal relationships among those who worked at the <u>Städtische</u> Oper lasted only until the beginning of 1933. In March of that year, brownshirted members of the SA (Sturmabteilung) ...

ES: What was that?

AS: *Sturmabteilung.*

ES: Oh, I see, that is again political ... it hasn't got anything ... I wasn't even around, you know. It had nothing to do with me there ...

[break in the tape as doorbell rings]

AS: *Nineteen thirty-three was the year when Schwarzkopf, a pupil at the Berlin Hochschule, "first heard decent singing", according to Walter Legge. She claims to have been only a very few times to the Berlin Staatsoper, ...*

ES: Yes, perhaps three times, in all.

AS: *... where she heard Frida Leider and Dusolina Giannini.*

ES: Yes, and I heard Erna Berger in *Ariadne* as Zerbinetta and I heard Lemnitz.

AS: *As early as November 1933, in his speech for the inauguration of the RKK (Reichskulturkammer) Dr Goebbels had explicitly declared what he was going to expect from all its members: "No one, however high or low, has the right to use his personal freedom, and that applies also to all creative artists". And to the Hitler Youth in their official paper* Will und Macht: *"Musical education is a political message to the whole nation, no longer the private business of the individual".*

ES: Oh, is it? Do you think anybody of us heard those speeches? Well, of course not.

AS: *Not very appealing statements, one would have thought, but they worked, and helped swell memberships of the junior, affiliated organisations to well over 50 per cent.*

ES: And he wants to say: "especially Miss Schwarzkopf" probably, you see.

AS: Yes, because the implication is to hurt her.

ES: What was it that Goebbels wanted? That what, music was a political ...

AS: *No one, however high or low, has the right to use his personal freedom, and that applies also to all creative artists. Musical education is a political message to the whole nation, no longer the private business of the individual.*

ES: Well, no it isn't, is it? Damn it all, to learn to sing is not really a political ... He should have tried, you know!

AS: *At this time, many first-class singers ...*

ES: I don't think Goebbels can have been that stupid to say that, you know.

AS: *That's what Goebbels declared.*

ES: *Ja*, I know, Goebbels can't have been that stupid to say that, that musical education is a political ... Oh, surely he wasn't that stupid, you see. I doubt that very much.

AS: *At this time, many first-class singers who were racially or politically unaffected by the new regime remained, or had since arrived, at the Deutsche Oper. Thanks to the experienced management, a good balance of voices had been maintained by the right kind of singers to fill all the roles in the house's repertory. Although the principal dramatic soprano, Elsa Lárcèn, was Swedish, the versatile lyrics and coloraturas were Aryans from the Greater Reich. Among them were four in particular with whom Schwarzkopf would soon be competing, in spite of her youth; for although protocol was involved in the formal method of promotion based on age and length of service, ...*

ES: Well, sure.

AS: *... it was sometimes possible to bypass one's seniors with sufficient protection ...*

ES: Oh no, my dear, you got hit over the stomach when they found somebody who was gifted and they didn't like it. My dear colleagues, marvellous as they were.

AS: *... with sufficient protection and the kind of determination ...*

ES: And what kind of "sufficient protection", I'd like to know. Where is it, what is that? Who? Who would that be?

AS: It's innuendo, isn't it?

ES: Now that is a big innuendo of something, something, isn't it?

AS: *... and the kind of determination that Schwarzkopf already seemed to possess.*

ES: He doesn't speak of the musicality, does he? That's all there is to it!

AS: No, it is all ambition and determination.

AS: *Some of the tenors and baritones at the Deutsche Oper, such as the lyric tenor Walther Ludwig and the Heldentenor Gotthelf Pistor ...*

ES: Whom we adored.

AS: *... (whom Schwarzkopf greatly admired), had extensive guest artist contracts for the Berlin Staatsoper, and for Vienna and Bayreuth. Karl Schmitt-Walter, an elegant, light-voiced baritone, was later to be of enormous help and encouragement to Schwarzkopf.*

ES: Yes, he was, namely to say that I should go to Ivogün.

AS: *Of the two principal basses, Eduard Kandl had been a member of the company since its beginning and was also one of its few* Kammersänger.

Karl Schmitt-Walter

ES: Well, there must have been quite a lot, you know. *Kammersänger* is not a very exclusive thing, you know, everybody got a *Kammersänger* in the theatre.

AS: *Schwarzkopf took her first step in the same direction as Rode when she joined the NSDAP a month after arriving at the Deutsche Oper.*

ES: Who? Who? I did?

AS: Yes.

ES: But I didn't – it was only after great things in '40 when I applied for it.

AS: *She had to sign a form stating that she came from an entirely Aryan family and had never been in any way connected with the Jewish faith; then, eight days later, she made another detailed declaration about the racial purity of her parents and grandparents, …*

ES: Everybody had to do it, so what? That was all – they had to be non-connected with Jews. It is quite true, but that it didn't mean a thing. We didn't enquire into

Wilhelm Rode

the lists, where we were born in Poland, what happened and, besides, I must laugh because Fröhlich is such a Jewish name, you know, but no, it wasn't really such a … everybody said "your grandmother's family one of…". Ah, God!

AS: *… completed in her presence by a Party official at the Deutsche Oper.*
It took two years before she was registered as a full member of the German Nazi Party, …

ES: Not before I registered, before I applied.

AS: *… and that was not ratified until nine months later, in December 1940, when she was sent her Berlin Party number and her* Arbeitsbuch *…*

ES: That is the thing. You were not allowed – that was the thing. I would not have been allowed to work any more. That was it – that's why I had to apply. My father said, "You do that because you have to sing, of course". Can you imagine, what a person, like my father, having been dismissed, what he has to go through then to say to his daughter, "Well, of course you do apply" – surely, it isn't done just not thinkingly, but he knew I didn't know anything about it.

[NB. Friedrich Schwarzkopf had refused to let the Nazis hold a political meeting at his school shortly before they came to power. He was dismissed from his job when they did achieve government, and he was not allowed afterwards to take a permanent teaching post. As another consequence Elisabeth was barred from entering a university (as she mentions earlier in her recorded comments) and instead she studied at the Berlin Hochschule für Musik. Her father was later sent to war zones, mainly on the eastern front, where his duties involved identifying those who had been killed in the conflict, notifying relatives and making arrangements for the return of the bodies.]

He had such a belief – both parents – that my voice, musicality, all of it – that was all that matters for them in life, wasn't it? Lily, you knew them. Nothing else mattered at all. And it wasn't ambition, it was really the belief in somebody being very gifted, which I now must say I must have been or else they wouldn't have given me all those roles in no time, you see. Beginners' roles, mind you, like the Lumpensammlering, and like Ida and like the First Boy – which was already a big part – in *Magic Flute*, not Papagena, First Boy.

AS: … *(a kind of Party log-book) that had to be deposited at the Opera.*

ES: What is that?

AS: That's the *Arbeitsbuch*.

ES: *Arbeitsbuch* – it could be, I don't know. I wouldn't know what it means, you see. One was permitted to work or one wasn't permitted to work, according if one had applied to the … Now, the thing which then follows, and sure it does follow, I didn't receive that then, whatever it was, *Partei* – what do you call a document, what would it be? A card, or something, and it didn't come and my father, in the meantime, was in Russia and my mother and I, we were terrified that it might not arrive and that they then by that might say I can't sing, and then, the irony of it all is that in Vienna, I was terrified that it *had* arrived somewhere. Ha! Really, so they would prohibit me there. No? It was really was frightened – *Furcht* – yes, fright. Oh God, this wretched thing hasn't arrived, what do we do now? With my father not there, what do we do now? Will they give it to you the next moment, you see? Well, they never did that, but in the meantime I really did make some career with Lieder singing and so on with [Michael] Raucheisen. And in Vienna, it was the same thing, for God's sake, you know, did this thing ever arrive? Hopefully it hasn't – it hadn't, but was it somewhere it should be – I have applied for it so somewhere there must be something on the way, still, in the war. Then, with me being in Slovakai, with my father being in Russia and my mother in Berlin and being bombed out, *ja da war nicht* – great much order in the things – was also not there. And later, if I wanted to take all there was in correspondence with me, I couldn't get into the flat any more – no, so there. And my mother, when she got out, she had that broken arm and could only wear one handbag in that right arm, the other one, which arm I don't even know, but she got out by that way. So we didn't take all writing stuff with us, and things, it wasn't done, and we had, you know, the people who had, perhaps you must have had in England, a bag standing by your bedside with the necessities in order of alarm, which you just had to jump down in the thing *Luftschutztasche*, you see. *Nah ja.*

AS: *The Opera House contracts normally ran from 1 August until the 31 July of the following year; ...*

ES: From when? First of August? Might have been. The holidays would have been only July, wouldn't it. It may have been, I am not sure, because one of them ran from First of September – now, wait a moment, when did the war start, at what month? The Polish war?

AS: August?

ES: First of August? Well then. We were on our way back from the holiday only, so it must have been some days later, the middle of September or the beginning of September. Is he talking about '39 there?

LR: In general, I think.

AS: *Well, he goes on to say, ... but with only three months to go before the end of the season, the agreement with Schwarzkopf covered only the forthcoming 1938-39 season.*

ES: Yes, well that's true. It is not quite a year, about eleven months. That's true.

AS: *Schwarzkopf's contracts were all annual until the one due to begin on 1 August 1943 which was for three years, but she never signed it.*

ES: Well, they didn't know I didn't sign it, of course not.

LR: That was with Böhm.

ES: Yes, that was with Böhm, that thing, yes.

AS: *In April 1938 she became a "Soprano (Beginner)" in the Deutsche Opernhaus, Berlin, to receive 2,400 RM a year paid monthly (about £12,000 in 1995 purchasing power) with an extra 2.50 RM (a comparable £15) if she sang twice in one day. She was obliged to give up to four performances a week "as cast", which meant singing any role the management chose to give her, but the payment for a second performance was stingy, because if that were the normal going rate, she would have to sing eight times a week.*

ES: And sometimes I very nearly did, you know.

AS: *Schwarzkopf had been engaged as a soprano, rather than as a chorus member, …*

ES: Well I auditioned for the soprano, I didn't audition for the chorus. Those were quite different auditions. Oh, how silly.

AS: *… so she was entitled to some consideration in the distribution of parts.*

ES: Oh no, you were not entitled to anything as a beginner the first two years, then sing what they said.

AS: *From her first full season of 1938-39, which began in August, she had to sing far more than four times a week and in a variety of small roles, some of which were desirable cameos.*

ES: Oh like what was? Maybe the *Lumpensammlerin* was rather … harder, harder, harder … maybe! [laughs] Oh dear.

AS: *The management did not force her at the outset of her career, …*

ES: And this is the way how it ought to be, even now. It was the ideal upbringing for a singer, and I have said it all my life, I was lucky to be in a big house as a beginner, because then I could learn all my craft and all those small roles which wouldn't kill me. Nowadays, you sing your first big role in the Met, you see and you are offered it for the next five years.

AS: *… and required her to learn only one new role a month.*

ES: Well, I learnt far more than one new role a month. They knew I learned it in no time, you see. And I learned and learned all the time, by the way, so there.

AS: *After her Wellgunde Schwarzkopf was already expecting to be given more named roles, …*

ES: Oh no. I wasn't. I was absolutely sure that I should sing my beginner's roles for the two years – not after those two years. Then I was expecting Adele, which they then took away from me, first of all for Paris and that was quite right because they don't go to Paris with the third cast, third range whatever, you know, they took the stars – and so, no, no not right.

AS: *Schwarzkopf was already expecting to be given more named roles, …*

ES: Do you know also what I object also to? That he repeats the name seven thousand times. It is not necessary, he fills the book with it. Is that as one does it? Oh dear!

AS: *… but her third one was a Rag Picker in* Evangelimann.

ES: Yes, that's the one with the Lumpensammlerin.

AS: *It cannot have suited her because she somehow managed to drop it …*

ES: I did what?

AS: *It cannot have suited her because she somehow managed to drop it …*

ES: I didn't. I didn't drop anything – I did what they said. If they dropped it, so it was dropped. I hadn't any say in what I had to do.

AS: *… and never appeared in Kienzl's opera again. Two other assumptions were quite good ones for a beginner: Esmeralda, the pretty Circus Dancer in Act III of* The Bartered Bride, *who has two decent duets (and whose dress was to make a totally unexpected appearance five years later); …*

ES: Why, after the bombings!

AS: *… and Adele's "Schwester Ida" in* Die Fledermaus, *…*

ES: … two sentences and then all ensemble!

AS: *… which Schwarzkopf positively hated because Ida has no solo line. There is only dialogue, and all Ida can do otherwise is to sing along with the chorus.*

ES: No, with the ensemble, my dear. That's all wrong, not with the chorus. There is an ensembling in "do-i-do, do-i-do, da da da" – that is ensemble. What has talk about it? I think I stop it, you know, it is too much rubbish. It is too much rubbish, for Christ's sake. First of all we'll have a … we'll do another hour on the chicken and then we'll leave it on the chicken hob! [laughs].

AS: Do you want to carry on, or not?

ES: Well, if that goes on like that we'll never finish until Christmas … now I mean just to … would it be fairer if I do read it myself now?

AS: It's up to you.

ES: Honestly, it isn't fair, you know … if that is … I would have to put big red things

Schwarzkopf as Esmeralda in Bartered Bride

under every line, almost. And then perhaps take it to pieces, from out of that then, but it is just so silly … or maybe I ought to write a critique about the book, you know. Lily – can you just turn the rice round a bit, just once, please?

AS: He was talking about Ida. *From the start, Schwarzkopf had her eye on the far more worthwhile Adele.*

ES: Surely every soprano has – you have to hear how many people are presenting to read the role to do, for a light soprano. Having her eye on – I mean that's what your teacher intends – you have to study this, that you have to study Gilda, you have to study this, you have to study Adele – that's the normal procedure of a singing teacher to say now you study this, not Constanze yet, but Blondchen yes, you see, things like that. Ah, it's so silly.

AS: *Her last role before the season ended was a rather spectacular one as Marie, the heroine in Lortzing's light opera* Der Waffenschmied *(The Armourer). Obviously she was being tested by the management to see how she might respond to the forthcoming season when she would be put through her paces. Nineteen performances in her first 28 weeks was below the usual average for an attractive young soprano at the Deutsche Oper.*

ES: What, what, what? Nineteen performances in 28 weeks? What is 28 weeks? It's a…

AS: Half a year.

ES: … *Zwanzig is fier, funf, … sechs, sieben Monate* – what are we talking about? Twenty … well, if only we count how many performances I did really …

AS: I don't know what he is talking about, 19 performances in the first 28 weeks.

ES: Nineteen in the first 28 weeks – much more, much more. She [LR] can give me the figure in a minute, and what is he talking about, 20 …

AS: I don't see the significance of 19 performances in the first 28 weeks, I don't understand what he is talking about.

ES: But I did sing much more than that – really! [laughs]

AS: Of course. *Naturally, though, she was busy learning other roles in preparation for advancement.*

ES: Oh, isn't that nice of him to consider that one did prepare roles for … you know.

AS: *In the following season of 1938-39 she progressed at great speed with 16 new parts, of which the first important one was Frasquita in the trio of gypsies from* Carmen. *The policy at both Berlin houses was for all operas to be sung in German, making for easier comprehension by the audience and for national pride in their language.*

ES: Silly, "national pride in their language" – so that the audience could *understand* it. Pride they are when you go and hear Goethe's *Faust*, OK, but only in the *oper* that is just to be understandable.

AS: *Hence Schwarzkopf's second important role was the extrovert Musette (Musetta) in* Die Boheme, *who moves from her impossible flirtations in Act II through the bitter quarrel with Marcello …*

ES: He is going to tell what it is! Look at that!

AS: ... *in the next act to tender sympathy at Mimi's illness and death in Act IV.*

The First Noble Orphan in Der Rosenkavalier *was Schwarzkopf's baptism in a Richard Strauss work, although it was going to take nine years before she reached Sophie, and 17 before she undertook the Marschallin. The Orphan was one of Schwarzkof's "quick home" roles of short duration in performance. The sopranos taking the three Orphans in Act I are sometimes called upon to change to terrified Faninal maidservants pursued by the Ochs retinue in Act II, ...*

ES: Sure, same persons.

AS: ... *and among Annina's tormentors of the Baron in Act III, ...*

ES: No, that isn't really true, because that was always the chorus; it isn't true. It was the chorus. And they would have complained if they wouldn't have had those – and they were not solo voices, they were just chorus.

AS: ... *but Schwarzkopf's contract specified "soprano", not chorus member.*

Likewise, the Duchess of Mantua's Page in Act I of Rigoletto *has a vivid, short solo engaging everybody's attention;...*

ES: Oh no, it engages the conductor's attention because it is what we call *Geschmissen*. In half a minute or 30 seconds, if you are wrong it is gone and is already false wrong: it is a role where you have go in, sing, bing, out you go! [laughs]. It was *Geschmissen*, gone.

AS: ... *and, rather later, the Woodbird's Voice in* Siegfried, ...

ES: Now that's quite important.

AS: ... *which is sung offstage, did not even require her to change into costume.*

ES: What a silly remark. It is so childish, you see, is it not? Oh my God Almighty. The man has nothing to do with the profession, really, because anybody mentioning that in the theatre would be ashamed, you know.

AS: *In all these cases, Schwarzkopf was able to leave the theatre early in the evening and, because they are all decent little roles, it seemed thoroughly indecent to her rivals that she was being favoured with them when she had been in the company for so short a time.*

ES: That I was favoured with roles that sent me home earlier than the other roles? Never in my life – things so, so silly as that, you know.

AS: *This is all part of the business of survival ...*

ES: What about, for instance, the singer in *Rosenkavalier*, now? Is that one of those roles, would you think? Oh dear.

AS: *This is all part of the business of survival in an opera company.*

ES: What?

AS: This question of being favoured.

ES: Well, I must say this has nothing to do with it. It is just unmentionable that – and I have never heard it in my life as an argument. Perhaps when the bombings came and one was led that one could still come home to a decent time because we were *Bomben* wards you know, in the opera, we younger people, wards over us. But to have an advantage over the others in reality – what, because one goes …

AS: *Other singers, especially the less favoured, are always quick to spot such advantages by one of their colleagues; and when that more talented (or more favoured) artist is considered to be on the same rung of the ladder, the more jealous the others become, female of female, male of male.*

ES: Yes, but that was never mentioned, that simply wasn't a reason, you see: we know that the more talented in that case, and that is what it is. And I wasn't the more favoured – it was simply because the – the directors of the theatre knew what they had. They gave it – they had the safety that the person could sing the next day a role which she hadn't even had a rehearsal.

AS: *An ever-widening variety of roles laid a firm foundation of Schwarzkopf's future successes, although at the time some of their musical and dramatic significance seemed negligible, if not rather tiresome, like the First Squire in* Tannhäuser, *although she was sometimes given the Shepherd in Act III as well, and that was always worthwhile.*

ES: The Shepherd in Act III? The Shepherd is from Act I to Act II. Lily! Hello! The *Tannhäuser*, please! [laughs] Yoo-hoo, we want the *Tannhäuser* score, please, the *Tannhäuser* score, please! It was from the Venusburg to make the changement into, what was it the first, … am I mistaken? Is it to this last act, is it to the shepherd boy … the changement is within the first act, from the Venusberg, the Venus mountain, to when they had found themselves on the green whatever, all the Tannhäuser and the friends and Wolfram and so on, isn't it? I haven't seen it for a long time, but that is what it is … Oh. Oh dear, make it …

AS: *We'll ask Lily to look it up. There was the other First Squire in* Lohengrin, *the unimportant Pepa in D'Albert's verismo shocker,* Tiefland *(popular with the Führer)* …

ES: What? Oh, I say, oh dear, that's why I sang in it – what the? … Sure, sure.

AS: *… and the minute role of Inez in* Il Trovatore, *waiting woman to the principal soprano.*

ES: Yes.

AS: *They nevertheless became the means by which Schwarzkopf accustomed herself to quick study, to continuous changes of makeup and characterisation, while it was sometimes necessary for her to make adjustments in her own role when singing opposite different colleagues. All this is the stuff of being a performer in a busy organisation running at fever pitch and with human temperament in abundance.*

ES: With what?

AS: *... human temperament in abundance.*

ES: In any theatre that would be, you know. If there weren't people with temperament, it wouldn't run in the first place, no theatre would. But is an observation which I have also made so far – that's a revelation, that is a revelation to observe human temperament! It is here, of course. Somewhere here [*Tannhäuser*] the scene is in the First Act! Not the Third Act – a nice part to go home early from, you see! [laughs]

AS: He can't even get anything right, can he? *In 1936 Norbert Schultze's* Schwarzer Peter, *subtitled "An Opera for Young and Old People", from a story based on an old German folk-tale, had first been given in Hamburg. Schwarzer Peter is the name of a German card game equivalent to Old Maid, where you must avoid being left with the named card, and the opera is a light-hearted work with clearly drawn, fantastic characters, ideal for Christmastime and a welcome change from* Hänsel und Gretel.

ES: Yes, it is.

AS: *Now, in December 1938, the opera had its Berlin premiere and performances continued intermittently until March.*

ES: How does he know? Has he read some of the critics, maybe, who described it such? Then he should say. "... as I read in the so and so paper as Mr so and so writes in his critique ..." Surely the clot hasn't ever seen it, or looked at the score, nah!

AS: *Lore Hoffmann ...*

ES: A wonderful singer, Lore, she was our marvellous Pamina, she was, oh yes.

AS: *... first sang Erika, a rich king's daughter and the heroine, which Schwarzkopf then took over for three nights.* Lily says four. *She has one delightful aria, "So schönen Blumen hast du" ("You have such beautiful flowers") and a love duet with Roderick, a poor king's son. Schultze conducted a few performances himself.*

ES: Norbert Schultze – he was the one who composed *Lili Marlene*.

92

AS: Yes, he is coming to that. *A few months before coming to the Deutsche Oper, he had composed a sentimental song that was hardly noticed at first but, in 1941, was broadcast from German-occupied Belgrade and immediately caught on, travelling round the world wherever there were soldiers of any nation, ...*

ES: That's not right, the Schultze opera was tinged, they needed something in place of *Hänsel und Gretel*. They couldn't play *Hänsel und Gretel* all the time.

AS: *... and soon becoming the internationally best-known of all wartime songs:* Lili Marlene.
   Early in her operatic career, Schwarzkopf exhibited many of the traits that were to become characteristic of her professional behaviour:

ES: What is that?

AS: *... full concentration on the matter in hand; absolute seriousness during rehearsals; intolerance of vulgarity; consideration for the conductor ...*

ES: Exactly – I would like to smear that round his face, you know.

AS: *... consideration for the conductor and director, ...*

ES: Consideration is not the word. I was in awe of the conductor, really in awe.

AS: *... but sufficient presence and determination to state her own case and argue it when given instructions that she considered unreasonable.*

ES: Oh no. There was no argument – you did what the conductor said, in those days. I only started arguing now, in the last ten years – I had to, you see – but then there was not a question of an argument, ever, with nobody. Not with the producer, certainly not with the conductor, of course not. Unheard of, you see. You would have been out of the theatre, the same moment.

AS: *This applied particularly to her contract, her salary and leave of absence, ...*

ES: That's a different thing.

AS: *... all of which became of such vital importance that they led her, for a while, to throw overboard some of her main attributes as a well-behaved member of the Deutsche Oper.*

ES: Like what?

AS: He doesn't say, does he? Then he goes on to talk about Hitler's territorial demands and so on, so shall we skip that bit?

Rupert Glawitsch

ES: Ah, yes.

AS: And then he says war was declared on 3 September in 1939 between England and Germany. *The next day was a Monday, when the sun rose on the first of more than 2,000 days that were to dawn before the end of the war …*

ES: The next day of what?

AS: Well it was the next day in September, 4 September 1939.

AS: *… in Europe left the "Thousand Year" Reich in ruins. On that rather special morning, 4 September, Elisabeth Schwarzkopf made her second recording of four duets from operetta with the popular Hamburg radio tenor, Rupert Glawitsch.*

ES: How did I know that it was a special morning – can you tell me that? What has it got to do with it?

LR: It has to be arranged long before, you cannot just arrange that day for a recording, it has to be set before.

AS: Well, he doesn't suggest that that was the case.

LR: But he suggests that you did it on that special morning.

ES: It suggests that we did it in spite of the war, we did those duets.

LR: And four duets it wasn't.

ES: No.

AS: It wasn't duets, you were singing independently, weren't you?

ES: What was I singing?

AS: *It was a single 12-inch disc of a potpourri from Franz von Suppé's* Boccaccio. *Another selection, from Lehár's* Paganini, *displays her voice as exceptionally strong and pure, at this stage in her career, and with the character emerging vividly. Her short solos and the duets are pretty, light and agile, but without the last degree of finish to the phrases. On top notes at ends of numbers the intonation is slightly suspect; but one instantly recognises that Schwarzkopf is the more interesting of the two artists, even though Glawitsch was a minor star and his operetta tenor's bright voice is by no means to be despised.* That's very nice of him!

ES: Yes, he was really very well known. They did those recordings on account of him, not with regard to me. Sure, he was on the radio very often, he was really quite somebody.

LR: Herbert Ernst Groh, who he mentions somewhere, he was on Electrola.

ES: Who was on Electrola?

LR: Herbert Ernst Groh.

ES: Herbert Ernst Groh – oh, I see. Was he in those recordings?

LR: He was an Electrola artist. And Glawitsch was a Telefunken artist – the recording was for Telefunken.

ES: Was it? If she says so!

AS: He's not saying it was Electrola, though – he's not suggesting it was Electrola.

LR: No, but he said that other record companies tended to use celebrated tenors like Herbert Ernst Groh, Walther Ludwig and Marcel Wittrisch.

AS: Where?

ES: Well, Walther Ludwig and Marcel Wittrisch were certainly more better-known, but he was on radio and so on, but he wasn't on the opera stage, that he wasn't, Glawitsch, I believe. He was only for, well, operetta, but not on stage. I wouldn't have known that he had been on the stage.

LR: In those days, people didn't run from one company to another to make recordings. They had a contract with one company.

ES: Yes, yes. Well I don't know, but …

LR: But I know because it was much easier to find out if an artist had made a recording for a company – nowadays you never know. They can be on Decca or HMV or RCA – they can be on anything. But those days they were staying on one company.

AS: I see what you mean – we are just coming to that.

AS: *Such recordings exemplify one of the methods deployed by Goebbels of jollying along the German people.*

ES: What has it got to do with – after all, who was Goebbels? When we did those famous operetta recordings with Ackerman, who was then jollying along whom? Can you tell me? Or Richard Tauber singing operetta all the time. Now what was that made in aid of to jolly along whom, politically? That's really lunatic, you know.

AS: It is, it is. *Competing record companies tended to use celebrated tenors like Herbert Ernst Groh, Walther Ludwig, Marcel Wittrisch or Richard Tauber, whose voices outclassed those of their respective sopranos. But on her debut disc Schwarzkopf, not yet 24, was Glawitsch's equal.*

ES: No, I wasn't. No, of course not. I wasn't yet with Ivogün, so I was really not ready, oh no.

AS: *Schwarzkopf began her first full season at the Deutsche Oper with the new role of Bertha in Weber's Gothic opera* Euryanthe, *a useful part in an awkward work that is somewhat out of fashion today. Then, after further developing her characterisation of Marie in* Der Waffenschmied, *she sang the other Marie in Lortzing's* Zar und Zimmermann *with Hans Wocke as Tsar Peter the Great.*

ES: Yes, a very good baritone.

AS: *Disguised as a carpenter, he discovers how other nations build their ships. It is a pleasant work and hers is an attractive role.*
   The First Boy in Die Zauberflöte *was Schwarzkopf's introduction to a Mozart opera, a part she held on to for as long as she remained at the Deutsche Oper, …*

ES: As long as I was slim enough, in reality. As the first boy, you know! [laughs]

AS: *... in spite of the fact that she generally avoided* Hosenrollen *(breeches parts). Then, in December 1939, she was cast as Barbarina in* Figaro, *a first step towards Susanna and the Countess.* Figaro *and* Die Zauberflöte *were so close to Artur Rother's heart that he conducted practically every performance.*

ES: He was the *Generalmusikdirektor*, so who should have conducted them?

AS: *Likewise, he took almost all the* Parsifals *and* Rings *in which Schwarzkopf was now singing Ortlinde, second voice among the warrior maids in* Die Walküre.
  In the spring of 1940 she sang Lauretta in Gianni Schicchi, ...

ES: But I think only once. How many times did I sing that, Lily?

LR: A couple of times.

ES: Did I? Do you mean twice? Or what? Can't have been much.

AS: *... with Hans Reinmar taking the old rogue's part.*

ES: Very famous baritone, that was.

AS: *Lauretta has the only "hit number" in this one-acter: "O mio babbino caro",* ...

ES: So what a revelation, Herr Mister! Ach.

AS: *... which Schwarzkopf was to record in 1949.*

LR: '48.

AS: It's incredible, isn't it!

LR: It *was* '48.

AS: *On 1 May 1940 there was a significant piece of casting, from her point of view, when she was at last given Adele in* Die Fledermaus.

ES: Which year does he say? 1940?

LR: 1 May 1940.

ES: Did I sing it 1 May 1940? So that was already – was I still under the beginner's contract? Or under the soubrette contract? Wait a minute. The beginner's contract went again from September '38 till September '39 till September '40, so I was still under the beginner's contract. It is quite so, but it is given to beginners when there, the other one isn't – you know, somebody is ill, or so, so they have to have a reserve, sure. *Ja*, that is what the other singers saw coming up, sure, and they didn't like it.

AS: *It was ideally suited to her vocal lightness and agility coupled with her flair for comedy. She was delighted at having been given it to sing at last, because the personal cachet attached to the character had become a sensitive issue and Schwarzkopf now hoped that her name was going to occur far more frequently on the Adele roster.*

ES: *Ja*, as then on Ida, which I did sing.

AS: *Evidently the management thought otherwise, because the Idas kept returning to her far more often.*

ES: Sure, *ja*.

AS: *She was to sing Adele only three more times, …*

ES: But every theatre would try out a youngster on a main part, rather than say, "Well you sing it wrong now" – that's all silly. No theatre does that, you know. Ach, he has no idea.

AS: *She was to sing Adele only three more times, with a final score of 22 to five.*

ES: What does that mean?

AS: Making it look like a football score, isn't it?

ES: What, what, what? *Wie ist das? Ich verstehe nicht* [I don't understand].

AS: Well, it means that you sang Adele five times and Ida 22 times.

ES: I see. We'd better look it up, Lily. I don't know, I don't think it is quite right, is it? I don't think I sang it that often – before the famous thing with Paris, you know, Act II Ida – I don't think so. We have it, on our numbers, *ja*. Where do I have this thing with the numbers?

LR: I don't know.

ES: Well, never mind. It wasn't five, I am sure. Well, never mind, *ja*.

CHAPTER THREE

AS: Right, *Chapter 3: Rising Star 1940-1942.*

ES: Ah, silly clot – star! It is so far from it, that – it can't be. You know, I wasn't singing *Traviata* or anything of the sort, for instance.

AS: *The Berlin Staatsoper and Deutsche Oper fulfilled their quasi-political functions under Goering and Goebbels respectively, …*

ES: What do they mean – the quasi-political functions? What does he mean by that, for instance? Indoctrination with the Nazi ideology or what? Or doing good opera performances? So was Covent Garden, so was Paris Opéra, so was Stockholm – what did they do? The same operas as we did. What had that to do with La Scala, or the Met? – they did the same operas as we did. What did they indoctrinate their public with, I wonder?

AS: *… and each vied with the other in producing works that appealed as much to their individual Party bosses as to the public.*

ES: Oh, come on! Honestly, it had to be a success and the public had to come, that was number one; if the public didn't come, that wasn't too good for any theatre, it wouldn't have been. Oh!

AS: *Hitler still involved himself with Bayreuth and continued to give the Wagner family all his moral and financial support.*

ES: That has to be questioned whether – I don't know it. But was it true that he gave it financial support? It's not my business to question that – but one can question anything he says, you see.

AS: *The Bayreuth singers, in that hot summer of 1940, were drawn exclusively from the Staatsoper thanks to Tietjen, whose Prussian operatic parish extended that far. …. The avidly pro-Hitlerian Jaro Prohaska, …*

ES: Jaro Prohaska, the famous baritone.

AS: *… a fine bass-baritone, was a member of the company: his neurotic wife, whose inclinations followed her husband's to excess, …*

ES: Her what? What was that?

AS: … *his neurotic wife,* …

ES: His *what* wife?

AS: Neurotic.

ES: Neurotic? Emotional?

AS: Neurotic – means very nervous, to the point of illness.

ES: Oh, I see. What has that to do with …?

AS: *… generally had to be carried out of the room in a faint if the Führer was present.*

ES: Oh come *on!* Ahh! How low does he sink, you know?

AS: *The baritone Herbert Janssen once asked her why she had a golden swastika on one hand, fastened by chains to her fingers and thumb.*

ES: Now that is a story that is really meant to be a funny story. It was a *Witz* [joke] from Herbert Janssen. I knew Herbert Janssen: he said it to make a joke, you know. It wasn't true.

AS: *"That is where the Führer kissed me!", she replied coyly, …*

ES: That was a joke – she was known – I didn't know her, but later on it was said that she was so Führer – something that surely she would have worn a thing where the Führer kissed her hand or whatever. Nah! But that is … you don't put that into a book, do you? Oh *no,* oh no!

AS: *… to which the normally courteous Janssen retorted: "A pity he didn't kiss you on the mouth!".*
By the end of the 1939-40 opera season in August, Schwarzkopf had sung a total of 37 different roles and was becoming recognised as one of the most promising young sopranos at the Deutsche Oper. In the few rather unimportant roles that she sang, her star quality shone through, and, if her acceptance at short notice into the company can be regarded as the first break in her career, an even greater one now followed. She was sufficiently well regarded by the end of her first full season to be cast as Zerbinetta in a new production of Richard Strauss's Ariadne auf Naxos.

ES: Yes – when was that, Lily?

LR: In '41 – September '41, as far as I remember.

ES: *Ja,* that's true.

AS: *The role was written into her contract for 1940-41, justifying an increase in salary to 9,000RM for the year, duly authorised from Goebbels's office.*

ES: That had nothing to do with Goebbels – somebody who does the finances has to authorise it, surely.

AS: The slightest chance he has to try and make it …

ES: Yes he does, with the presence of the Führer, with the presence of … it is so dirty I cannot say.

AS: *In a short space of time she had been handed a plum part that others have waited years to try to catch.*

ES: No, there was none other available at the moment, I tell you – it wasn't there. Beilke didn't sing it – she would have been the one – Irma Beilke – but she did not sing it. I don't think – maybe it wasn't her – maybe she couldn't, I don't know. But there was none I know who could have been doing it, while I was there.

AS: *Zerbinetta is a flighty member of a Commedia dell'Arte team, the only woman among four men, who believes in taking as many lovers as possible and getting as much out of them …*

ES: Why doesn't he come in with Hitler any moment again, maybe? The Zerbinetta character, you know!

AS: *… as she can before dropping each in turn when she tires of him. The vocal role parallels and parodies this philosophy in stratospheric coloratura, and demands absolute precision in the acting and an artful sense of humour. Zerbinetta is a delectable little minx. To succeed in the role, the singer must focus all the attention on herself whenever she is on stage, even to the exclusion of Ariadne, the prima donna.*

ES: First she must sing them. And that's what I didn't – you should have heard Ivogün about that. She heard the performance – the first one – and she said, "It was terrible".

AS: *This requires star quality, which you either possess or you don't. Schwarzkopf did. She achieved a public success but confessed, much later, that "it was a dreadful indiscretion" to have attempted it.*

ES: It was what? A dreadful?

AS: Indiscretion.

ES: To what? What does that mean?

Irma Beilke

AS: … *a dreadful indiscretion to have attempted it.*

ES: Yes, well I did … indiscretion – is that the word? Stupidity, I dare say it is. Indiscretion means whether they reveal a secret, isn't it? Or has it got another meaning?

AS: It's the wrong word, isn't it?

ES: It's the wrong word, of course. Indiscretion – it has nothing to do with being indiscreet, has it? To sing that role – it was simply stupid. A wrong judgement by the people in the opera, to think that I could already do it.

AS: *After the first and second performances on 28 and 30 September, a short announcement rather than a review, as was the custom, appeared in the* Berlin Lokal-Anzeiger *of 1 October:*
   Richard Strauss's Ariadne auf Naxos *is now in the repertoire of the Deutsche*

Opernhaus. The main parts in Hans Batteux's new production of this most charming chamber opera are taken by Bertha Stehler ...

ES: Bertha Stetzler.

AS: He says Stehler.

ES: We have to look that up, Lily, in the programmes. I think it is Stetzler – I think – I seem to remember, Bertha Stetzler.

AS: *... as Ariadne, Elisabeth Schwarzkopf as Zerbinetta, Henk Noort as Bacchus and Karl Schmitt-Walter as Harlekin. Musical direction is by Artur Rother.*
   Maria Ivogün, the most famous portrayer of Zerbinetta since Selma Kurz, ...

ES: Not true – since Selma Kurz, not at all. It was the – the first performer was – oh God, in Munich. It was not her, at all.

AS: Well, he says, *... its creator in the opera's second version.*

ES: It had nothing to do with Selma Kurz

LR: Stetzler.

Schwarzkopf with Schmitt-Walter in *Ariadne auf Naxos*, Berlin, 1940

ES: Stetzler, T-Z. What is the name of that woman? We could ask Tubeuf, he would know – the very first Zerbinetta. That was the famous one against everybody had to compete – not Selma Kurz. Selma Kurz was not terribly musical, you know – she did those fantastic trills which Ivogün envied really. She cried all those trills and … she may have sung it in Vienna after all, but the famous one was …

AS: Was it Rose Pauly?

ES: No, no – Pauly was a dramatic soprano, she was an Elektra – sang the role at Covent Garden. Elektra – no I won't tell you the story – oh no, better not! From Walter – oh, no! Ach. We'll find it – I'll ring Tubeuf – he knows it.

AS: *Maria Ivogün, the most famous portrayer of Zerbinetta since Selma Kurz, its creator in the opera's second version, was in the audience that night. Ivogün had first joined the Deutsche Oper in 1925 but retired from the stage in 1933 to teach in Berlin. She was married to the celebrated accompanist Michael Raucheisen, the Gerald Moore of Germany.*

ES: Yes.

AS: *Karl Schmitt-Walter came to the Deutsche Oper in 1935 as a leading baritone with a light, musical voice and very clean production; …*

ES: That I would have to verify – with the son of Schmitt-Walter who wrote me a letter – I've got a letter there from him, not now, but from previous times whether that is true, because we don't want to have wrong dates in this, you know – we'll have to verify that, Lily.

LR: 1935.

AS: *… he was on good terms with Rode, who protected him against pressure to join the Nazi Party, which in fact he never did. Before singing Harlekin opposite Schwarzkopf in this* Ariadne, *Schmitt-Walter had been impressed by her voice and personality and by her generally professional manner. He also came to the conclusion that her vocal technique could and should be greatly improved, …*

ES: He simply said: "You can't sing!" [laughs].

AS: *… and it is likely that he had already prepared the ground for what he was going to say to her after the performance:*
"Look, my child, you have a good voice, and are gifted. That's obvious. But you are going to need to learn how to sing all over again. I'm going to introduce you to Madam Ivogün!".

ES: I must have told that story quite often.

AS: *This was a name to conjure with, especially for a young singer; and when Ivogün heard in Schwarzkopf all the necessary requirements and ability for Lieder singing, she agreed to take her on as a special pupil providing she was willing for her voice to be taken apart and rebuilt, note by note, in the right way.*

ES: That's true.

AS: *Otherwise the great teacher would only be wasting her time. Many years later, in 1987, shortly before Ivogün died, Schwarzkopf asked her what this first Zerbinetta had been like. The celebrated singer answered, "Simply terrible! Here was a girl with great talent and no knowledge of technique at all".*

ES: Yes, that is true. I must have said that many times, you see.

AS: *Schwarzkopf agreed willingly to the proposition, though again there was the need for extra funds to pay for these singing lessons, but strings were pulled and they were soon authorised by high authority in the Reichstheaterkammer.*

ES: What, what, what, what? What is this? That it has to so with paying them? I didn't have to pay much of them – I paid some, I really didn't. She taught me for whatever – I don't remember that I paid at all, you know, I must say, no, no.

AS: He says, … *again there was the need for extra funds to pay for these singing lessons, but strings were pulled and they were soon authorised by high authority in the Reichstheaterkammer.*

ES: Meaning what?

AS: *Strings were pulled …*

ES: That they paid in addition to have lessons?

AS: Yes.

ES: And the theatre didn't even know about it, you know. That was my private pleasure to go and be taught. Oh no, that is so untrue, it cannot be. It is also not … *wie sagt man?* – *üblich* [usual, common practice] – it's not …

AS: Well, that is damaging, isn't it?

ES: It is damaging – the theatre had nothing to do with my having singing lessons.

AS: There was no higher authority?

ES: Oh *no*. Never, *ever*, you see. That *is* really damaging, yes. The theatre had

105

nothing to do with it. Besides, I think one would have to keep it from the theatre to so that oh, she is still learning. Ah no, you see.

AS: You wouldn't have wanted to advertise the fact, would you?

ES: No, not at all … Oh God, no! No!

AS: *It cannot have been easy for her to go on singing at the Opera as usual, while taking lessons which often contradicted what she had already been taught and was still doing.*

ES: Sure, it wasn't.

AS: *Schwarzkopf sang even more Zerbinettas between then and early December, with a guest artist replacing her for one other performance: apparently no other soprano in the company was able to sing the role. She then gave a single performance the following March which turned out to be her last in Berlin. She was a very ambitious girl.* Here we go again. *Even before her first audition, she realised that the Deutsche Oper would serve as a useful platform from which to jump into lucrative recitals, films and recordings whenever she had free time.*

ES: Oh no! This really is a mischief – what do you call it?

AS: It is evil, isn't it?

ES: Yes, it is evil. Ah, what do I say to that now? It really is evil. It *is* evil. And it boils down that he has no, or doesn't want to have, any inkling about a musical-minded person … rises, works, thinks even, you see. I never, ever do think, well the contracts were nothing, besides the Ivogün Rauscheisen had me making those contracts when I had to fight also for my summer one, surely. But that doesn't mean if I wasn't ambitious, it doesn't mean that I was a dumb girl who sang everything for nothing in the opera house – I had to have a more fee for the next step as a … sure, and Ivogün and they were the ones who said, "No, no, no, don't let yourself be swindled out of what is your due". Ivogün was the first one, you see. Not then, it was before Ivogün, but even so, anybody known to us would have said, "But, for God's sake, don't be dumb, you know, you must ask for a rise in fee now you have another status – so surely you should have another … Wouldn't anybody have done it? Everybody is, in a free … now let us say, when the fee isn't – *wie sagt man da?* – systemised, this year this, the next year that. In our profession they have to battle for their rise in fee. They always have – and they have now. Now, it is what the agents do; in those days, those letters we had to do alone. Not the agents – nowadays it is the agents doing that same thing. Oh No!

AS: It's a very horrible insinuation, isn't it, really? … *a useful platform from which to jump into lucrative recitals, films and recordings whenever she had free time. Her attractive personality and appearance, coupled with a certain magnetism and a truly professional determination, all contributed to her swift rise from the ranks; but Wilhelm Rode was disturbed because she was always pestering him for more important roles.*

ES: No, I never asked for a role at all – they *gave* them to me, they *gave* them to me. They came and they said, "Well, do you feel you can sing that – Sophie or something later, you see, we want to give". I never had to ask for a role, never – they were given to me.

AS: *An interesting vocal relic of Schwarzkopf's Berlin days …*

ES: And that applies to the Marschallin – it was Karajan and Walter who said, "Now you have to sing the Marschallin". I said, "Are you crazy, I can't do it". The role came even later, or you must sing Elvira – are you crazy, you know, everybody? They came and said, "Yes, you must do that" – Ohhh! It is the whole idea, the whole concept of a profession – well, he doesn't know it, I mean I have to excuse him, he simply doesn't know what goes into a professional way, you know.

AS: Well, if that's the case he shouldn't be writing a biography.

ES: Well he doesn't know it.

AS: *An interesting vocal relic of Schwarzkopf's Berlin days exists on CD, singing the Second Rhine Daughter, Wellgunde. It comes from a broadcast performance of* Das Rheingold *from the Deutsche Oper on 24 May. Is that on CD, Lily? It's on LP, certainly.*

LR: Yes I think so, on Melodram.

AS: *In the excerpt heard, Alberich's voice is omitted altogether, making it a potpourri of the Rhine Daughters' trios in the first scene.*

ES: In order to please Goebbels, again? – Why doesn't he insert that now? I'm waiting for it.

AS: *Hilde Scheppan, First Lady in the Beecham* Zauberflöte *recording (when Schwarzkopf was a chorus-member), and the mezzo, Marie-Luise Schilp, …*

ES: She was our mezzo for all kind of minor roles, you know, Marie-Luise Schilp.

AS: *… make up this trio. It is a fine performance in which the orchestra of the Deutsche Oper plays extremely well under Artur Rother. She now began to aim even higher in her determination to reach the top in the shortest possible time, …*

ES: Oh no!

AS: *… taking her successes calmly in her stride, striving, even pleading to be cast in roles that she felt she was well able to tackle, …*

ES: No, I did never, never ever did I plead for any role, never, ever. I haven't ever, not in my life, not with, not with Walter, not with anybody at all. In fact I always had to say, "Sorry, I cannot do that, I cannot do that". It is so much against what I did, so the contrary.

AS: *... even though her senior colleagues were convinced that they were rightfully theirs. In her own mind, Elisabeth Schwarzkopf was on course to becoming a prima donna and she was not going to let anyone stand in her way, least of all those who abided by opera house protocol.*
.... Unfortunately, this attitude was not universally accepted; nor did it endear her to other sopranos, especially Irma Beilke, ...

ES: No, because she should have been, you know, if she could have she would have done Zerbinetta. Maybe it eluded her, I don't know but she did all our ... she did a lot of Susannas and she did all kinds of those roles really. But surely she was perhaps not a ... she was Papagena in Walter's thing – yes, sure, but I don't think she would been ... I never asked her whether she would have done Zerbinetta, I don't think so, but never mind.

AS: *... especially Irma Beilke, Konstanze Nettesheim ...*

ES: Konstanze Nettesheim was a pupil of Ivogün's and she was Pamina, a wonderful Pamina.

AS: *... and Lore Hoffmann.*

ES: Lore Hoffmann was a wonderful Pamina, all those the Zerlina, the Pamina, the what have you, Susanna, everything – a wonderful singer and actress – charming, and to look at beautifully, the Nuri in *Tiefland* and all this.

AS: *They were all older than she, and, having reached an intermediate rung of the ladder before Schwarzkopf's arrival, were naturally vexed that she had so suddenly bobbed up, almost from nowhere, to compete with them. And when she was obliged to take the unimportant roles, known as* Wurzen, *three or four other young sopranos in this category, like Ruth Jahncke, also resented her.*
.... The singers in an opera company, while they still have a chance of promotion, are always striving for attention, advancement and popularity in competition with those of their own Fach *at least, ...*

ES: Sure, it isn't nice for an older one to see there comes somebody who will perhaps be better – it is not easy to fathom, surely, it isn't, you see.

AS: *... and, for the sake of peace, a delicate balance has to be kept in relations between them all. The maintenance of this balance is generally in the hands of several members of the management from the intendant down to the stage manager and the wardrobe mistress and dressers, many singers' confidantes. In less than a year, Schwarzkopf* *had managed to upset this equilibrium among the sopranos with whom she worked because she wanted immediate results, whereas most of the others were prepared to plod on in the hope of gradual advancement.*

ES: Oh come on! What can you do against this – I mean you can tell them ten thousand times that wasn't my way at all. What can we do there – we cannot work – what is it? It is really against my whole make-up. It is. If I would have – tell me *one* part I asked to do. I'd like to know that. What could that have been? Nah! What? One role which I would say, "Oh I want to do this role, really – I'd like to do that". It wasn't – I don't know one. And not in Walter's time, either – or songs, not in … none, never ever ask for anything, no.

AS: *During rehearsal one day, a female singer in the company, who was carrying a property riding whip, …*

ES: What was that?

AS: *During rehearsal one day, a female singer in the company, who was carrying a property riding whip, …*

ES: Oh that was Margret Pfahl. She was the Traviata and all those great roles – wonderful – I took everything I possibly could artistically from her in … for the Rosalinde, for the recording, even so many years after, because she was – she must have been an Austrian – with an enormous charm and really a perfect Rosalinde, if there ever was one. Oh yes, but she was also a beast, a fiend.

AS: *… slashed at Schwarzkopf's legs …*

ES: No, she didn't slash at my legs, she slashed at my stomach to …

AS: *… because she was dominating the rest of the cast by standing too far downstage.*

ES: No, I wasn't dominating them – she just wanted me to be back on stage, you see, and it was in a role which I hadn't got rehearsed – it was for *Wildschütz*, it was in *Wildschütz* – Ach!

AS: *One wonders whether this may have been more than a lone individual's public protest.*

ES: That what?

AS: *One wonders whether this may have been more than a lone individual's public protest.* It wasn't public, was it – it was a rehearsal?

ES: No, it was in a performance – she did the main role. In *Wildschütz* there is a soprano with a very difficult aria to sing and she was marvellous in that and we had

Margret Pfahl

… there's an ensemble where we all stand in front, everybody, four people you see, singing, and I was just obviously one half yard too far forward so she took her riding thing and whipped me over the stomach, sure, she did. So there.

AS: *In October 1939, …*

ES: What good is it that I protest violently now – can we – do those protestations bring anything of the truth to the audience? Will it?

AS: Well, I feel that if we simply correct the factual errors which we know are wrong, then I think that goes a long way to reducing his credibility in all these other ways – I do believe that.

ES: *Ja*, but I would like the public to know that, for instance, I did never ask to sing anything at all – it was given to me, because people said, "Oh well, *she* can do that". They suddenly saw – ah there, there's somebody who can do that and so I got roles which I had never known in my life – they were given to me: you do that, you do that, you do that, always. Even in Walter's time. I didn't ask for the Marschallin, I didn't ask for the Countess, they gave it to me because they … you can surely do it. They were there, you see. I did not dare to ask, I didn't dare – it is so wrong that I was rather fresh you know. I did never – I was frightened to, I was frightened to ask anything. I was frightened most of my life in the theatre, in front of the conductor, the colleagues, everybody. It is all rubbish if I analyse how I behaved – Oh God, oh God, oh God, oh God, she will be against me, that will be against me, sure, you see. And the greatest fright was that the conductor was content with what I did musically – you know, for God's sake I hope it will be all right, that was all the time there. Yes. With De Sabata, with Karajan, with Furtwängler, the later years, it was through my life; Fischer-Dieskau not being perhaps satisfied with what I did singing beside me and perhaps not liking it or so. *Nah ja*, yes. Perhaps I made it look differently, but that is what it was, *ja*. And only …I don't, well … Shall I ask Miss what's her name for an interview again with the BBC? – Would you like to do a new interview with me? – what's that infamous woman there?

AS: C**** W*****.

ES: Yes, C**** W*****, when I was so unsuspecting doing it, you see.

AS: I know.

ES: From the correspondence, it's really very – I apologised, early and so on, I couldn't have, whatever… really totally unsuspecting what of anything, you see. But of course if I do an interview now it will … I will carry it away and I cannot contain myself – be calm that I will not be able to, I am sure I won't, no. So that wouldn't be so good, no. *Nah ja*. How does it go on from there? God, we have done very little, have we?

AS: *In October 1939, when Schwarzkopf considered she had become sufficiently established in the company to do something original, she appeared barefoot on stage as the Young Shepherd in* Tannhäuser, *instead of wearing the footwear provided. There were ructions over this, but Schwarzkopf innocently replied that she had done it before and felt more comfortable with bare feet.*

ES: I remember, but faintly, only very faintly. But the thing was the Shepherd had to wear the kind of leather soles with those leather thongs being wound up one's legs and they came off and I had to take them off and not to fall, you see, if you were not used to that, and they were not tightly drawn – it simply was uncomfortable for me, I don't know. You see, I am falling on stage over those leather bands, ribbons which – there, that was it, I know. Yes, it comes to me – I had forgotten about that – it was also not important, very silly. Why shouldn't the Shepherd Boy be barefoot, in the first place?

AS: *She was given both verbal and written reprimands by Oberregisseur Dr Batteux, who fined her 100RM, a substantial sum for a first offence – Rode reduced it by half. In the following season she was also often in trouble. On one occasion she was late back for a* Fledermaus *speech rehearsal with the excuse that she had run all the way from the film studios at Babelsberg.*

ES: I was never in Babelsberg. The film studio where I was was in the town – it is not true.

AS: *… (that was indeed a very long way!) and had to get bandages for her feet …*

ES: Ah, silly – this couldn't be done, you know. That was quite silly, quite silly. I couldn't – you'd have to go for three hours in order to run from Babelsberg to Charlottenberg – that's really idiotic.

AS: *… and had to get bandages for her feet because they were so sore. A goody-goody who keeps quiet and always does what she is told in an organisation like an opera house, especially one with political affiliations, is not likely to attract much notice. She will merely be taken for granted and may not even be thanked for her loyalty. Schwarzkopf was determined to be noticed as often and by as many people as possible, …*

ES: Oh no, come on!

AS: *… and she certainly achieved this intention. Yet the Deutsche Oper always had first call on her and, …*

ES: That is really mean because I had to behave as well as I possibly could, regarding to the situation of my father, that was, for God's sake, not to do anything which would be against the …

AS: *Yet the Deutsche Oper always had first call on her and, for the time being, she knew she must not endanger her security there.*

ES: No. I mustn't endanger anything, you see. It was the situation with … that is the overriding thing, that my father – don't do anything which they will hold against you, you see, like little things. Maybe I did protest against those shoes – I don't know, I mean I really don't know. And it is so – where do they draw those silly things – from tales of my … of the other singers, maybe.

AS: Well, let's look at the footnotes – Chapter 3, I can't find it immediately.

LR: Page 262.

ES: Yes, you know, singers, when they know somebody has a big success, they are prone to do terrible things. I remember once in Vienna when the men …

AS: Oh, it's supposed to be the BDC Elisabeth Schwarzkopf file, that's what it says.

ES: *Was ist das?*

AS: The BDC file.

LR: Berlin Document File.

ES: What is that? Why is this in a document? Why is this kind of thing even in a document?

AS: Is this the material that Dr Ritter is going to get hold of?

ES: Yes.

AS: Thank God for that – then we'll learn the truth.

ES: Yes, yes.

AS: As you say, it is probably some sort of tittle-tattle from another singer.

ES: Do you know that, at one time or other in Vienna, Walter – they told Walter that I had an affair with Schöffler and he believed it.

AS: Who was Schöffler?

ES: Oh, a great baritone, you see, but I met Schöffler on stage, he was our …

AS: Oh, Paul Schöffler?

ES: Paul Schöffler, yes, but honestly, it was … but Walter believed it for some time to come, and we didn't speak for quite some weeks – we didn't speak, you see, until he really saw that – and they apologised. But people will do that, and singers will do it. Yes, to keep the other one back.

LR: It says Berlin Document Centre, US Reichskulturkammer File on Elisabeth Schwarzkopf, 1938-45.

ES: *Ah, du wirst weinen* [It makes you weep.]

AS: Well, if Dr Ritter can get hold of these documents and prove that this is distorted, then, then there is a case …

ES: Well, what can he do, if it is in there? We don't know where it comes from – it may have been coming from Beilke, or from any of those singers.

AS: It must surely quote a source, mustn't it – they must quote a source, surely.

ES: Well I don't know, I wouldn't know – I have no idea. Maybe they do. Maybe, you see. Ah God! [laughs] What was this latest thing there? What I did, what did I then do?

AS: It was just a general remark about your determination to be noticed as often and by as many people as possible. *Her first ambition was to be cast as a middle-ranking soprano at the far more prestigious Berlin Staatsoper, …*

ES: Me? Never. There was never the question of it. After all, I had done the audition there, then I was in that Opera – I was a member of the Deutsches Opera House – that was it.

AS: *… although Tietjen had rejected her one indirect attempt to approach him.*

ES: What was that?

AS: *… although Tietjen had rejected her one indirect attempt to approach him.*

ES: I don't know about that – maybe.

AS: *She also had aspirations to appear annually as a guest at Bayreuth, …*

ES: [laughs] It sounds grand, does it not? Really!

AS: *… with all that that involved; …*

ES: Like what, as what, for instance? There was only the Rhinemaidens, what might have been my cup of tea for me then. Oh God Almighty! No, of course not.

AS: *… but the determined attitude which she displayed towards her female colleagues, coupled with her casual manner towards the intendant, inevitably resulted in decisive action being taken against her.*

ES: What attitude to the, for the colleagues? That word determination I hear all the time, you see. And surely I had no casual manner against the things – I couldn't afford that, I had to be polite and really doing what I possibly could, you see.

AS: *Whether it was a case of her having arrived 20 minutes late in the Opera House (fine 20RM) …*

ES: When was that?

AS: Doesn't say.

ES: It should say, because it may have been in the war when all the windows were broken and we had to first of all clear whatever there was in the road and then walk to the underground, not being punctual at all, and I had to go by underground, there was no other means, you see. And do you think I was going to be late with having to sing all those roles – how would I have learnt my roles if I was late at rehearsals? Not even I, who learned very fast, could have done it. Oh no. That is …

AS: *... or having left a rehearsal early and without permission, Schwarzkopf was still bothering Rode, ...*

ES: Pity they don't say when that was.

AS: *... and his disquiet at her apparent immunity from his control is clear from letters in the RTK file.*

ES: From whom? Who was that? Rode? Ah.

AS: *Nor did he misread the situation, which amounted to a good deal of interference over his head, allowing Schwarzkopf to enjoy support from highly placed persons in the Reich Ministry, constantly undermining his authority.*

ES: Oh no! Why would I have left rehearsals, with all that singing I had to do? What do they think I did? You know. Well, that's an insinuation which – whom should we ask now about that? What can one do?

AS: It will be in the papers, hopefully.

ES: *Ja.*

AS: *Rode's anxiety over Schwarzkopf is revealed in his correspondence with Ernst Keppler, Leiter (Chief) in the Theatre Division of the RKK, ...*

ES: What is he?

AS: (Chief) *in the Theatre Division of the RKK, ...*

ES: *Reichskulturkammer* – what is he – a Chief?

AS: A Chief in the Theatre Division. ... *when he tried to save face by asking for support from somebody senior to himself in the Reich Ministry, though not in highest authority.*

ES: Who did? Rode?

AS: *Although Rode may have displayed some weakness by admitting his inability to control Schwarzkopf, ...*

ES: Oh, come on!

AS: *... he insisted upon taking credit for having instantly spotted her talent at the only audition she gave them, straight from the Hochschule. Thereafter he had nursed her along and put up with her behaviour because, he admitted, he had great faith in her ability.*

ES: Isn't that nice? Well you can say that about anybody, you know, but how can you prove it?

AS: *Rode told Keppler officially how he had made it clear to Schwarzkopf that, for the time being, she must go on singing the smaller roles although she was being groomed for several of the more substantial ones.*

ES: And when was that? Does he give any year? Because if it was after my first recitals, then there was this question of not adhering to the contract, where Ivogün said that you must go and sing so they are not left, but you mustn't, cannot, you needn't sing under your own name – it's against the contract. Ivogün – you see, who was also a member of, had been a member of the opera – not of that one, though she did also sing there, the Staatsoper, but she knew what was, what was the usual thing. And they were very jealous that I had those successes in the Beethovensaal with Lieder singing – three sold-out halls. You see – Beethovensaal, not little somethings, but the Beethovensaal, which is *the* big concert, I mean Lieder hall, not the Philharmonie, but the Beethovensaal. And of course they didn't like it – they wanted to put me back, you see.

AS: *There were, after all, other sopranos to consider, but Schwarzkopf had decided to ignore this. So Keppler interviewed her in order to put over this point forcibly and directly; the fact that he got no further than Rode had done seems to indicate that Keppler was equally impotent when it came to disciplining Elisabeth Schwarzkopf.*

ES: How nice! [laughs]

AS: *She maintained afterwards that this had nothing to do with politics; rather, that she understood how to get round Rode (and apparently Keppler too) in order to further her career in the acquisition of roles and contracts that would secure quicker promotion.*

ES: What can you do about this? Come on, I think we had better leave it. It is too terrible, you know. What can we wish on to that man? What can one do? Have a ripe old age and enjoy your all your funds now? Maybe he will come to his senses and see what he has done, you know. Maybe somebody – but people, of course, of my age are no longer there, most of them. Schubartis dead, all the people who were there, Halle, all those colleagues of mine are no longer there whom I could … Walther Ludwig is dead – his wife is still there, I could ask her, for instance, but they are all dead. They are safely out of the way for Mr So-and-so, you see. Oh dear. It is what you call a *Hundling* – a hound. *Ja.* And the word "fairness" really is no longer in existence, anyway. Is it?

AS: Not in this, anyway.

ES: No, *nah ja.* Well, I wonder what's coming.

AS: *On 7 June 1941 Schwarzkopf and others took part in a benefit concert for Marie van Bülow in the Berlin Meistersaal. Hers was the major contribution, and included Frau Fluth's aria from* The Merry Wives of Windsor, ...

ES: For whom, Marie von Bülow, with a "w"? Well, I don't know who she ever was – who was that?

AS: Don't know.

AS: ... *included Frau Fluth's aria from* The Merry Wives of Windsor, *Johann Strauss's* Voices of Spring ...

ES: Yes, I very often sang that, yes.

AS: ... *and three groups of Lieder. There were five songs by Schubert, six by Schumann and, most importantly, for the first time in public, she sang five of Hugo Wolf's Eichendorff Lieder. She was accompanied by Michael Raucheisen.*

ES: Well, I see. That is hopefully true. I can't remember it. Is it anywhere, in the things I did there?

LR: We have a programme for it ...

ES: On the what, 7 June, they say, 1941. Well that must have been a few months after I had lessons from her and I think I took on with her technique very fast because I can only have been in it after the Zerbinetta, which was when, again?

LR: It was in '40.

ES: '40, and after that – what?

LR: September.

ES: So let's assume that I went to Ivogün immediately, which might have been the end of September, beginning of October, so in order to sing then the Frau Fluth, which I didn't sing before Ivogün and the Wolf I didn't sing before her, and Raucheisen didn't accompany me before I had lessons with ... it can only have been a few months, actually, which would be astonishing to alter one's technique already to that extent, you know. But maybe I did that – who knows? There you are. OK. It can't have been otherwise because we have the date of the Zerbinetta, and that alters, that sets the whole dates, really, doesn't it? OK – now what?

AS: There's a little bit of talk about France, now. *Germany's military successes in Europe had led to the fall of France in 1940. There was a need for some appropriate publicity in the occupied countries to demonstrate the established musical culture of the German people. In addition to those in Belgium, Holland and elsewhere, one of the most substantial was in May 1941 at the Paris Opéra, when the pro-German dramatic soprano, Germaine Lubin, sang Isolde to Max Lorenz's Tristan in an otherwise German cast, conducted by the young and brilliant Herbert van Karajan who was to be seen in Paris from time to time, directing either opera or concerts.*

ES: What, then, already? I doubt that. Well, never mind, I can't help that, you see. There's a big question mark on that – we'll have to look at the Karajan book, whether there's anything about it. Well, he would have looked in that book, wouldn't he? Presumably? Whether that's right? I don't think he would dare to put a Karajan remark wrong! Would they? Because they have all the money to sue him!

AS: *On this occasion he played the* Horst Wessel Lied *before the opera's* Vorspiel. *Wilhelm Furtwängler, his senior, refused to participate in such highly charged missions. The music, he maintained, must come first, not competition with his rival, about whom he was so paranoid that he was able to refer to him only as "that man K".*

ES: That he must have got from me, because …

AS: It is quite well known.

AS: *Previous Goebbels-sponsored musical tours and reciprocal events in Italy were not nearly as lavish as the three-week so-called "goodwill visit" to Paris by a total of 400 artists and staff in several prestigious works from the two Berlin opera houses. There was fierce competition among the singers, not only for selection but for roles.* Die Fledermaus *was scheduled to open the tour with seven performances; its farcical Viennese plot and marvellous score would appear lighthearted, charming and not provocatively* deutsch *at all. That was the thinking behind the choice of opera, but it was scarcely reassuring to the vanquished population of the French capital.*

ES: Well, never mind what with all this, now. Anyway, I didn't sing Adele – if he means … I did not. That's wrong with Mr Segalini in the first place – he hasn't done his homework, you see. Though it is very nice that book, but he says frankly Adele, but I did *not* sing Adele. I can't help it, I can't say white was black when black was white.

LR: That's in the letter from Schmitt-Walter – it also says you sang Ida.

ES: I am sure.

AS: He makes the wrong conclusion. *Far from being impressed with Goebbels's public relations exercise, the Parisians were highly indignant when they found out that* Die Fledermaus, *billed in German, would be sung in German and that audiences were to be restricted to local German civil and military personnel.*

ES: I don't remember that, no.

AS: *Worst of all, it was to be staged at the Palais Garnier, the Opéra, one of France's proudest cultural bastions, which had been commandeered for the occasion. The event could not have been intended to woo the French through art, as a terse comment in* Le Figaro *on the day before the premiere made clear "La Chauve-Souris de Johann Strauss va être donnée a l'Opéra. C'est bien la première fois qu'on entendra une operette au Palais Garnier".*

The first night, on 17 September 1941, was in the presence of the German C-in-C in Paris, General von Stülpnagel, with Ambassador de Brinon representing Vichy (German occupied) France. Walter[sic] Ludwig, the graceful Mozartean lyric tenor from the Berlin Staatsoper, sang Alfred, ...

ES: Not Staatsoper, he was on the Städtische Oper, he was our tenor, our resident, our main Mozart tenor.

AS: And wait for it! ... *and Schwarzkopf was cast as Adele.*

ES: Well, there you are! You see.

AS: *She should have considered herself very fortunate indeed, especially as her chief rival, Irma Beilke, had taken the role when the production opened at the Deutsche Oper in 1938.*

ES: It simply is not true. It simply *is not true.* What can you do? And I have asked Mr Segalini – I said you have done me a great injustice in putting that without really doing your homework in this thing because it just simply wasn't and I've asked the Deutsche Oper and they have no programmes of the Paris appearance any more, so we can't – I wonder where I could find out. I wonder who is still alive – because that *is* really rather important in the eye of the public, if they think – ah, in Paris she was given, which I was not – I was very pleased to do anything at all that it was in here, you see.

AS: I suppose the Opéra wouldn't necessarily have any records because it was a German visit.

ES: They haven't – they say no, but I must ask them again, you know.

AS: What about the Berlin – do they have any records?

ES: Well, I have asked them already and they say no, they have no programmes and the Opéra itself in Paris has no records.

AS: Well there must have been some kind of ...

ES: I'm going to ring Tubeuf, see whether he's there.

END OF RECORDING

PART 3

NOTES ON PAGES 42 TO 225 OF THE BOOK

As indicated in the Introduction, this section notes just some of the incorrect material contained in the second and by far the larger part of the text of Alan Jefferson's book, *Elisabeth Schwarzkopf* (pages 42 to 225). This second part was the subject of a second set of reading sessions that took place between 6 and 10 July 1996. An audio recording of these sessions was not made, and comments below derive from notes written by me at the time of the sessions. As before, these sessions were also attended by Lily Reenvig.

A.S.

Page 42. [The 1942 Paris visit, discussed at the end of the tape-recorded section].
"... she has confessed to being furious at her 'demotion' to the non-singing role of Ida on subsequent nights and made her feelings abundantly clear by kicking off a shoe that made a hole in the cyclorama ..."
ES: This incident took place much later, in Berlin, in the third or fourth year at the opera house.

Page 42.
"By her own account she was relegated to the smallest roles under the pseudonym of Maria Helfer..."
ES: No, this name arose after the recitals with Raucheisen, in late 1942 and early 1943 when Ivogün advised me not to sing small roles under my own name.

Page 49.
"...December 1942, when she joined a Berlin Artists' Tour with two concerts in Prague and two for the Waffen SS on the Eastern Front. She received only 375DM in cash for them all, a paltry figure that would suggest generous expenses."
ES: These were concerts for the troops, and we were not paid. You *had* to do it!

Page 50.
"... and the Czech Lina Baarova. Goebbels was so infatuated with the gorgeous Baarova, his long-term mistress ..."
ES: Her name was *Lida* Baarová.

Page 50.
"... Of the five [films] she [ES] is known to have made, only the first has survived, called Die Drei Unteroffizieren *..."*

121

Schwarzkopf with Michael Raucheisen

ES: The title was *Die Drei Unteroffiziere*.

Page 58. [Berlin in 1944].
"She sent Rode three lists of operatic roles… Notably absent are a few, like Zerbinetta, which she had clearly put behind her …"
ES: No, the voice had changed. I was no longer a coloratura.

Page 77.
"After the Second World War began in 1939, Legge initially remained with Columbia…"
AS: He was an employee of HMV and had been seconded to Columbia and Beecham.

Page 81.
"By the time Schwarzkopf signed her exclusive contract with Columbia Records…"
AS: For legal reasons the contract was with the Swiss Turicaphon company.

Page 81.
"Telefunken, for whom she had made four 78rpm records in 1940 …"
LR: It was in 1939 and 1940.

Page 85. [The first Columbia recordings]
"Her only other studio recording from this opera [Entführung*] was the* 'Traurigkeit'
aria made a week later, which was not considered suitable for release."
LR: It was released on 78rpm, LP and CD.

Page 93. [With Walter Legge]
*"Schwarzkopf ... heard records of Fritz Kreisler and Artur Schnabel, whose inspired
instrumental playing could be made to sound like singing."*
ES: Kreisler, yes, but I heard no Schnabel records at this time.

Page 93.
[ES quote] *"...It can really show what a legato is, which is very different for
singers..."*
ES: ...which is very *difficult* for singers...

Page 100.
*"Schwarzkopf and Otto Klemperer had seldom worked together, but in September
1949 she accompanied him on a tour to Australia."*
ES: No, Klemperer was then based in Sydney: my accompanist throughout the
tour was Margaret Schofield.

Page 102. [The first performance of Strauss's *Vier letzte Lieder*].
"Schwarzkopf knew Flagstad well and was able to give her some moral support ..."
ES: I was not present at this rehearsal.

Page 103. [1950 performances of Bach's B minor Mass under Karajan].
*"Legge began a recording with the Vienna Symphony Orchestra ... and seized the
opportunity of engaging Kathleen Ferrier ... her final illness and death prevented it
from being finished".*
LR/AS: There was no such recording, only live performances, one of which has
been issued complete on CD.

Page 105. [Karajan in Milan]
*"Schwarzkopf has often stated that she demanded three weeks to rehearse a new role.
Her request met, she would then put on a magnificent show ..."*
ES: These were Karajan's demands, not mine!

Page 110. [A 1951 London performance of the closing scene from *Capriccio*].
*"... it was accepted wholeheartedly as an absolute delight which her complete
recording, three years later, was to confirm."*
AS: A recording of the closing scene from *Capriccio* was made in September 1953;
the complete recording was made in September 1957.

Page 110. [May 1951].
"... her maiden performance of Strauss's Four Last Songs, *which curiously, she was
not to sing again until 1954."*

AS: She gave a performance in Hilversum May 1953 and made her first recording of the work in September 1953.

Page 112. [Furtwängler and the Beethoven Ninth at the 1951 Bayreuth Festival].
"The work was also going to be recorded ..."
AS: There was no intention then of making this performance commercially available; it was only issued in the absence of a planned studio recording after Furtwängler's death.

Page 117. [Bayreuth in 1951].
"All such hopes were dashed by her declaration that she was not going back."
ES: It was only because of the clash with the Salzburg Festival that I did not return.

Page 119. [*The Rake's Progress*, 1951].
"A week after Lucerne, and with Rake rehearsals in between, she was in Milan for a very special performance of the [Verdi] Requiem ..."
LR: It was in Venice.

Page 119.
"The vocal soloists were Ebe Stignani, Giuseppe di Stefano, Cesare Siepi – and Elisabeth Schwarzkopf."
LR: The tenor was Tagliavini, not Di Stefano.

Page 120.
"Legge always wanted Schwarzkopf to create the principal role in an operatic world premiere ... his persuasiveness resulted in her being cast as the faithful heroine;"
ES: No, I was a late replacement for an unnamed singer.

Page 121. [*The Rake's Progress*, continued].
"...when Stravinsky was on the rostrum for rehearsals, Leitner stationed himself behind the composer so that he could give cues to the singers ..."
ES: No, Leitner took the rehearsals, and it was at the first performance under Stravinsky that Leitner sat in the front row and surreptitiously gave cues.

Page 122. [More on *The Rake*].
"If Schwarzkopf had expected Anne's music to be specifically tailored to her voice, she was disappointed".
ES: As a late replacement I had no expectations.

Page 123. [*Rosenkavalier* in Milan].
"The cast had a strong Viennese slant, with Lisa della Casa ..."
ES: Della Casa was Swiss.

Page 125. [A 1952 *Messiah*].
"This was the first of these performances, in French as Le Messie, *under the eminent Swiss composer and conductor, Robert Denzler."*

ES: It was sung in German.

Page 126. [Orff's *Trionfi* with Karajan].
"*... Carmina Burana, to a libretto based on erotic Latin and Greek verses, in which she did not sing ...*"
ES: Yes, I did!

Page 126.
"*... Trionfo di Afrodite, with the role of the Bride specially written for Schwarzkopf,*"
ES: Surely not!

Page 127. [Tippett's *A Child of our Time*].
"*... Walter Legge, who the previous year had been unsuccessful in persuading Tippett to take up the post of chorus master for his new Philharmonia Choir ...*"
AS: The Philharmonia *Chorus* was not formed until 1957.

Page 129. [1953 Wolf recital with Furtwängler].
"*... Furtwängler had insisted on having the piano lid open, spoiling the balance from some seats in the auditorium ...*"
ES: There was nothing wrong with the balance: it was the slow tempi!

Page 132. [Recording with Karajan in 1954].
"*... it was not until a year later that Schwarzkopf returned as Leonore, recording the Act 1 scena 'Abscheulicher!' on 78. Having been excluded on LP, this aria has emerged on CD ...*"
AS: This recording was first issued on LP and then reissued on CD.

Page 133.
"*...this uncharacteristic role [Leonore] heralded the second phase of new ones under Karajan's direction, which also included ... Marguerite in* Faust *in February 1954.*"
LR: *Faust* was conducted by Artur Rodzinski.

Page 133.
"*Karajan rounded off 1953 by persuading her to sing Pamina in a broadcast for RAI Milan of* Il Flauto Magico *...*"
LR: This broadcast took place in Rome.

Page 137.
"*The Legges were championing Karajan in his love affair with Eliette Mouret...*"
ES: An absurd suggestion!

Page 139. [*Troilus and Cressida* premiere, December 1954].
"*... she only had a few recitals in North America which ended a month before the first night.*"
LR: There were many recitals on a tour which lasted from 16 October to 5 December.

Page 140.
"On the first night at Covent Garden in December 1954, with Schwarzkopf and Legge among the audience ..."
ES: No, we were not there.

Page 141. [Re Karajan].
"In spite of his apparent lack of interest in French opera, remembering those doubtful Mélisandes under Rodzinski at La Scala ..."
ES: The conductor was Victor de Sabata, not Rodzinski.

Page 142. [Re *Figaro* in March 1955].
"He [Otto Ackermann] had also accompanied her sympathetically in the first (mono) version she made of Strauss's Four Last Songs *the previous year, after what was apparently her first public performance, under Fritz Reiner at a concert in Chicago."*
AS: The recording took place in 1953; and here Jefferson contradicts himself, since on Page 110 he suggests that ES sang her first *Four Last Songs* under Paul Kletzki in Vienna in May 1951.

Page 143.
"There were no Salzburg or Lucerne Festival dates in 1955 ..."
LR: There was a Lieder recital with Gerald Moore at Lucerne on 16 August.

Page 144.
"Then it was back to Milan for five performances of Die Zauberflöte *at La Scala in December [1955], this time in German ..."*
LR: These performances were sung in Italian.

Page 144.
"Cantelli was killed in a plane crash at Orly Airport the following November, at the age of only 35."
AS: Cantelli was 36 years old at the time of his death.

Page 145. [Karajan, 20 June 1956].
"... Schwarzkopf was there with Karajan in a concert which turned out to be his last as conductor of the Philharmonia Orchestra..."
AS: Karajan's last Philharmonia concert was on 1 April 1960.

Page 145.
"This performance of the Four Last Songs *was issued on CD in 1990, Schwarzkopf's seventy-fifth birthday year, to which she strongly objected ..."*
AS: This performance was issued with ES's approval: the version with Karajan to which she objected was a "pirate" recording of a 1964 performance.

Page 145.
"Then it was on to the delights of Lucerne, to sing songs from Wolf's Italian Liederbuch [sic] with Fischer-Dieskau ..."

ES: We sang the complete set.

Page 146.
"The 1956 stereo LP Rosenkavalier *was a tremendous success ..."*
AS: This performance was not issued in stereo until 1961.

Page 152. [Summer 1959].
"After a few performances of the Countess and Fiordiligi during June, she had no engagements during the summer except for two appearances at Lucerne ..."
LR: And one at Scheveningen.

Page 153. [Beecham's *Messiah* at Lucerne in August 1959].
"...during a final chorus rehearsal ... Putting down his baton gently but emphatically, he said quite quietly ..."
ES: It was during the concert itself that this incident took place.

Page 154. [Re Beecham].
"He conducted the Philharmonia only once ..."
AS: It was twice – the very first concert in October 1945 and the 1959 Messiah.

Page 159.
"Schwarzkopf gave her first public performance of Countess Madeleine in Capriccio *at San Francisco, under Böhm, in May 1960".*
LR: This performance took place in Vienna.

Page 162. [A quotation about an unnamed soprano attributed to Rudolf Bing, apparently recounted by Martha Mödl and then quoted in *The Last Prima Donnas*, by Lanfranco Rasponi, Gollancz, 1984].
"I can forgive her for having worn a Nazi uniform and for taking an American colonel as a boy friend right after the war, but I cannot swallow the fact that she then married a Jew".
ES: This is a nonsensical third-hand quotation!

Page 163. [Karajan and Philharmonia concerts once again].
"When Herbert von Karajan became conductor of the Berlin Philharmonic after Furtwängler's death in 1954 he was no longer giving concerts with the Phiharmonia..."
AS: Karajan became conductor of the Berlin Philharmonic in April 1955. On page 145 Jefferson has already referred to a Philharmonia/Karajan concert that took place in June 1956, and as noted previously, Karajan in fact conducted his last Philharmonia concert on 1 April 1960.

Page 166. [ES in Chicago, November 1961].
"There should have been three Elviras, but Schwarzkopf, still suffering from London flu ..."
ES: I was suffering from hepatitis.

Page 169. [ES as Adele in *Der Fledermaus*].
"... she had sung Adele in Fledermaus *at the Deutsche Oper (nowhere else) ..."*
ES: I also sang Adele in Prague. AS: As noted in the tape recordings, Jefferson alleged earlier in his book (Page 41) that Schwarzkopf also sang Adele in Paris on 17 September 1941, a suggestion that she strongly refuted.

Page 170. [Giulini's Verdi Requiem recording of 1963].
"But her voice combined with theirs less successfully than with De Sabata's all-Italian cast in 1951."
AS: The De Sabata recording was made in June 1954.

Page 171. [The 1965 Salzburg Festival].
"... and although Così *stayed in the programme, the American soprano Evelyn Lear had been preferred as Fiordiligi."*
ES: In fact I cancelled!

Pages 176/77. [Chapter 15 – After Karajan, 1964-1968].
"King Karajan went his own way...."
"By the summer of 1964, the Legge-Schwarzkopf partnership with Karajan had broken up ..."
ES: It had petered out in 1960.

Page 179. [George Szell and the *Four Last Songs*].
"Now Schwarzkopf was to sing for the first time under the awesome George Szell ..."
LR: ES had sung the *Four Last Songs* with Szell on at least two occasions before, the first being September 1956 at the Lucerne Festival.

Page 179. [ES and Glenn Gould].
"Legge thought that they would make an intriguing partnership ..."
ES: The suggestion for a collaboration came from Gould.

Page 180. [ES and Glenn Gould].
"The three rapid, spiky Ophelien-lieder ..."*
ES: Only one is rapid, the others are slow.

Page 180. [*Don Giovanni* at the Met, January 1966].
"After the first performance it was given out that Schwarzkopf was ill ..."
ES: I was ill, with sinusitis.

Page 181. [*Rosenkavalier* at Barcelona in December 1966].
"Schwarzkopf indisputably possessed the firm line when she made the recording 12 years earlier."
LR: It was exactly ten years before.

Page 182. [The Gerald Moore farewell concert, February 1967].
"... two words in a Haydn vocal trio were altered to 'O! wollte Gerald nun weiter

spielen!'"
ES: It was in fact "O! wollte Gerald *nur* weiter spielen!".

Page 182. [Schwarzkopf and Moore].
"... they gave their last conventional recital together at the Festival Hall in May [1967]."
LR: Geoffrey Parsons was the pianist on this occasion.

Page 183. [ES at a Covent Garden gala on 15 October 1957]
"She sang one Wolf Lied ..."
ES: I sang the "Willow Song" and "Ave Maria" from Verdi's *Otello*.

Page 189.
"She was living uncomfortably with a husband who made life miserable for everybody around him."
ES: How does he know!?

Page 190. [Walter Legge].
"... but he was still able to pun whimsically on the title of a Wolf Lied: 'Wandl' ich traurig von Book to Book'".
ES: This song is by Brahms.

Page 191. [March 1979].
"... were preparing for the last concert of all, on the 19th, in what she had determined was to be her future home-town of Zürich."
ES: This was not planned as the last concert: others were cancelled after Walter's death.

Page 192. [WL after the last concert].
"... 'You know, you're a bloody marvel!' he said to her with a huge grin ..."
ES: He actually said, "You're a bloody *miracle*".

Page 193. [After WL's death].
"Then there were Legge's last wishes to be fulfilled. He wanted his ashes to be put to rest near Hugo Wolf's grave in Vienna's Central Cemetery, and this was done following his cremation in Zürich on 25 March."
ES: They were not his last wishes: it was my idea, which in fact it did not come to fruition.

Page 196. [Teaching].
" ... while a promising Polish soprano, Dorota Jorda, has on Schwarzkopf's strong recommendation received grants for further study in Zumikon."
ES: Not true. I take no money from any pupil, and sometimes pay their hotel expenses. [In fact the grant was made by the Elisabeth Schwarzkopf/Walter Legge Society for Jorda's travel expenses only].

Page 196.
"Her transitions into and out of middle voice, head voice and supracuti ..."

ES: The word is "sopracuti".

Page 198. [1983].
"... and in the same year she became a life member of the Vienna State Opera, and was granted honorary Austrian citizenship."
ES: I became an Austrian citizen in 1947.

Page 209. [Re a 1964 *Rosenkavalier*].
"The skirmishes and skittishness with Octavian the morning after, and her coyness with Baron Ochs, struck an unconvincing note with many critics."
ES: This was at the request of the producer – and rightly so!

Page 209.
"In 1965 Schwarzkopf muses gently on the wretched Ochs after he has gone. 'Da geht et hin, der aufgeblasne schlecte Kerl' ..."
ES: It is in fact "schlechte".

Page 210.
"... but extended her arm in his direction, as if to say 'To be continued, mein Leib!'"
ES: It should be "mein Lieb".

Page 210.
"In 1954, Herbert von Karajan was principal opera conductor with the Philharmonia Orchestra for recordings ..."
ES: Not as such!

Page 210.
"Schwarzkopf's Fiordiligi is essentially serious, vocally assured throughout; she is uncomfortably prissy and affected at the opening of her first scene ..."
ES: As she should be!

Page 210. [Re "Per pieta"].
"... though the rather 'cooing' tone she uses here is not to everyone's taste."
ES: This is the head voice, without which you would not be able to sing Mozart!

Page 211. [*Così* in Milan, January 1956].
"... at the intimate 600-seat Piccolo Teatro in Milan ..."
ES: The theatre is called La Piccola Scala.

Page 212. [Dorabella with Carlo Franci, 1961].
"... sometimes making it impossible for her to articulate clearly (the acacciature suffer particularly in this respect)."
ES: The word is "acciaccature"

Page 216. [The first Lieder recital]
"On 9 May 1941 she gave her first solo recital, with Raucheisen again, in the Berlin

Beethovensaal".

LR: There were four recitals with Raucheisen, on 29 November 1941, 26 December 1941, 12 January 1942 and 13 February 1942.

Page 217.

"Schwarzkopf's wartime recitals were complemented by the concerts she gave for German troops, sponsored by the Propaganda Ministry, which comprised items like Strauss waltzes, Solveig's Song from Peer Gynt *and "Summertime" from Gershwin's* Porgy and Bess ..."

ES: These were troop entertainment concerts, the equivalent of the British ENSA concerts. I did not sing "Summertime" at these concerts: I learned this song after the war when I sang for American troops.

AS: It would in any case seem highly unlikely that a song by a Jewish American composer from an opera written for black singers would be acceptable to the Nazi authorities!

Page 221.

[The confusion between ES's 1956 live recording of Strauss's *Four Last Songs* with Karajan, which she allowed to be published, and the pirated 1964 performance (see reference to Page 145) is again repeated. On this occasion Jefferson suggests that ES "grudgingly agreed to the disc's release" and quotes her criticism of what was in fact the 1964 performance.]

Page 223.

"Schwarzkopf sang only a few songs from Wolf's Spanish Song Book *at ad hoc recitals. But she and Fischer-Dieskau performed the complete Song Book together at Lucerne in 1956 and Carnegie Hall, New York in 1964."*

LR: Both these performances were of the *Italienisches Liederbuch*.

HORST WELTER
DIRIGENT

VORM. DOZENT AN DER
STAATL. HOCHSCHULE FÜR MUSIK
FRANKFURT/MAIN
MUSIKDIREKTOR IN BAD ORB i. R.

TELEFON 06052-2401
AM KLINGENTAL 54
XXXXBAD ORB
63619

den 8.1.96

Frau
Kammersängerin Prof. Dr. Elisabeth Legge-Schwarzkopf
Rebhusstr. 29
CH-8126 Zumikon

Sehr verehrte,liebe Frau Kammersängerin!

In der heutigen Ausgabe der Frankfurter Neuen Presse steht
ein Aufsatz, der Sie als begeisterten Nazi bezeichnet(ich
lege ihn bei). In Ihrem freundlichen Brief vom 16.11.93
schrieben Sie mir, Sie würden sich freuen, von mir zu hören.
Nun, von dem was ich aus unserer gemeinsamen Studienzeit in
Berlin weiß, kann ich den Bericht nicht unwidersprochen lassen.
Mit Bestimmtheit kann ich sagen, daß Sie niemals die Leiterin
des NS-Studentenbund an der Berliner Hochschule waren.Dieses
Amt hatte Herbert Klomser inne(der war vielleicht ein Nazi
und hat dafür in seiner künsterlischen Laufbahn büßen müssen:
während des Krieges war er anfänglich in Wien als Bariton en-
gagiert, mußte nach dem Krieg an einem kleinen Theater wie
Heidelberg wieder anfangen, ich war mit ihm befreundet und
weiß, daß er nach dem Krieg sich von alledem distanzierte).
Wir waren damals jung und begeisterungsfähig und natürlich
(ich mit eingeschlossen) waren wir - wie der überwältigende Teil
des Volkes) begeistert, was 1935 um uns herum geschah.
In den NS-Studentenbund waren wir mehr oder weniger gezwungen
eingetreten. Wir kümmerten uns zur Hauptsache um künstlerische
Fragen, denn man studiert ja schließlich nicht Musik an einer
der größten Musikhochschulen Deutschlands, um irgendwo zu ver-
sauern, sondern um Karriere zu machen. Ich halte den Artikel
für Töricht und lächerlich und Sie können darüber denken wie
der berühmte Mond, den ein Hündchen anbellt.
Zu den übrigen"Vorwürfen" kann ich nichts sagen, nur finde
ich die Behauptung, daß Sie "nicht die übliche Lehrzeit an
kleineren Bühnen haben durchlaufen müssen," einfach lächerlich.
Auch die Erwähnung Ihrer britischen Staatsangehörigkeit mit
quasi vorwurfsvollem Augenzwinkern ist lächerlich. (wenn Sie
einen emigrierten Russen geheiratet hätten, wären Sie heute
Russin!).,Ich habe auch einmal gelesen, daß Sie eine polnische
Sängerin seien, weil Sie im damaligen Polen geboren sind!
Ich schreibe Ihnen das, weil ich nie Parteigenosse war und
1935 aus der SAausgetreten bin (auf die damals einsetzende
Hetze gegen unseren "Abgott" Wilhelm Furtwängler hin) um diesem
Brief mehr Nachdruck zu verleihen. Sie dürfen nach Belieben
davon Gebrauch machen(falls Sie das überhaupt nötig haben)
Wenigstens ist diesem blödsinnigen Aufsatz ein reizendes Foto
beigefügt, das beinahe an die "Elie" von damals erinnert.
Ich benütze die Gelegenheit, Ihnen nachträglich und nicht
weniger herzlich zum 80 .Geburtstag zu gratulieren (ich bin
in diesen Tagen 82) Mit den besten Wünschen für Ihre Gesundheit
bin ich immer der Sie bewunderte

(Horst Welter)

Letter from Horst Welter

Translation

Dear Frau Kammersänger!
In today's edition of the Frankfurt *Neuen Presse* there is an article that states that you were an enthusiastic Nazi. In your kind letter of 16.11.93, you said that you would be pleased to hear from me. Now, I know as we were studying together in Berlin, I can say that I cannot let the report go without contradicting it. With certainty I can say that you were never that leader of the National Socialist student association at the Berlin Hochschule. That office was held by Herbert Klomser (who was perhaps a Nazi and for his artistic career he had to suffer: during the war he was engaged as a beginner as a baritone in Vienna, then had to begin again at a small theatre in Heidelberg: we were friends, but after the war he distanced himself). We were at that time young and enthusiastic and naturally (me included) we were – like the overwhelming number of people, enthusiastic about what happened around us in 1935. We were more or less forced to join the student association. We concerned ourselves mainly with artistic questions, for we didn't study at one of the greatest Hochshules to stagnate somewhere unknown, but to make a career. I think the article is silly and ridiculous and you can think about it rather as the well-known moon that a dog barks at.
As far as the usual "accusation" is concerned I cannot say more, but I find the assertion that you "didn't have to spend the usual time in the smaller stage" simply ridiculous. Also the mention of your British nationality with quasi-reproachful winking is ridiculous. (If you had married a Russian émigré, you would today be Russian!) I have also read that you were a Polish singer because you were born in what was Poland at that time! I write to you that, because I was not a party member and in 1935 left the SA (at that time came the hounding of our idol Wilhelm Furtwängler), so as to give to more emphasis to this letter. You can use it as what you wish (if you have the need). At least enclosed with this stupid article is a charming photo that almost reminds me of the "Ellie" that I remember. I use the opportunity belatedly but no less warmly to congratulate you on your eightieth birthday. (I am now 82). With best wishes for your good health, I am always your admiring,

Horst Welter

Horst Welter was born in Frankfurt in 1914. He studied at the Hochschule für Musik in Berlin with Paul Hindemith and Kurt Thomas and specialised in choral, orchestral and opera conducting. In 1937 he worked as a repetiteur in Cottbus and then moved to Karlsruhe. After the second world war he became a lecturer at the Frankfurt Hochschule für Musik in 1955 and then, from 1967, music director in Bad Orb.

Masterclass at Forum Les Halles, Paris, May 1988,
with unknown pianist

Evening with Richard Baker, Guildhall School of Music,
London, 15 November 1990

Masterclass in Stuttgart, April 1995

Masterclass in Stuttgart, February 2003

Daphne Kerslake, Elisabeth Schwarzkopf and Sir Peter Pears, Zumikon, Switzerland, September 1984